TEACHING SCHOOL

A book for anyone who is teaching,
wants to teach, or knows a teacher

Revised edition

Eric W. Johnson

National Association of Independent Schools
18 Tremont Street, Boston, Massachusetts 02108

Contents

	Preface	v
1.	Order	1
2.	Interest	8
3.	Spirit	11
4.	Discipline	16
5.	Teaching the Basics: Instruction	27
6.	Teaching the Basics: Discussion and Mastery	41
7.	Dealing with Written Work	48
8.	Planning a Year and a Unit	54
9.	Planning a Class Period	57
10.	Study Skills	62
11.	Homework	68
12.	Organizing and Managing the People	77
13.	Organizing the Place	82
14.	Selecting, Organizing, and Managing the Materials	88

Contents

15. Organizing the Time   97

16. Evaluating and Testing the Performance of Students   101

17. Using and Misusing Standardized Tests   109

18. Making and Grading Your Own Tests   115

19. Marks and Comments   123

20. Reports to Students and Parents   130

21. Keeping in Touch   138

22. Getting Your Own Teaching Evaluated   149

23. Testing and Evaluating Your School   155

24. Education for What?   162

       Index   165

Preface

A cynic said, "Education is casting false pearls before real swine." Well, perhaps, in a few places, with a few people. But to me teaching is as noble, challenging, stimulating, and rewarding a job as one can set one's mind and heart to — except on rainy Friday afternoons and during the month of February.

This book does not set out to analyze the American education system or make either sweeping or carefully modulated recommendations for reform. Yes, I have read *A Nation at Risk,* published in 1983, and the score or so of studies and reports that followed. Many were excellent, but most of them, unfortunately, concentrated on the high school. I am thankful for this recent upsurge of thinking about our schools and for the growing realization that the strength of our nation, and of our world, depends on education, and that education requires teachers who are well recognized and well supported.

This book does set out to tell, in definite and practical ways, how to teach school in a classroom, how to know if you are doing a good job, and how to improve the school of which your classroom is a part. Teachers, or people thinking of going into teaching, will reject what doesn't work for them or for them in their school.

I taught for about thirty years in public and private schools. I also performed various administrative tasks, even spending four years as a school principal. After being a principal, I climbed steadily down the administrative ladder and spent most of my time as a classroom teacher of grades 4-12.

As I go about in both public and private schools, I see some teachers who are leading overstimulating lives of not so quiet desperation. I see others who have become habit-ridden, tolerating circumstances they see as unchangeable and responding with boredom and resigned adjustment tinged with cynicism. But I see still others — perhaps the largest number — who are trying energetically and successfully to do a good job. They keep their enthusiasm and their self-confidence but are always on the lookout for ways to do better. They recognize and are stimulated by recognizing that a sound education gives strong grounding in the basics, enthusiasm for life and learning, and the desire to be useful, productive, and considerate.

Books on education usually fall into one of two categories. One group brilliantly promotes a radical point of view or method that works for two or three years of system-defying, life-flinging effort on the part of the authors before they leave the classroom and take to the typewriter. The other group expounds, in textbook format, the elements of education, with lots of objectives, overviews, sections and subsections, summaries and study questions.

I have, however, discovered one especially readable, practical book on schoolteaching: *Points Picked Up: One Hundred Hints in How To Manage a School,* by Abbie G. Hall. Because it was published in 1891, it's a little out of date; I am sorry that Abbie Hall is not alive today to revise it. Her first hint is "Begin school as if you had just heard good news and took pleasure in imparting, and keep this up all day." Her last: "Honor your School Board that your days may be long in the land in which you are teaching." A few other choice hints:

2. If you would keep a bright pupil out of mischief give him enough to do.

3. To teach is not to simplify every step until there is no real work for the child to do.

11. Every thing that is explained to a pupil which he can find out for himself robs him of so much education.

26. When something funny occurs in school don't be afraid to laugh. It is frequently better to laugh than to scold.

41. Use suggestions instead of commands.
54. Discipline should aim at improving the character.
84. Do not scold and never threaten.

Who have I written this book for? I like to think that anyone who has any interest in education might find parts, if not all, worth exploring. But I have had foremost in mind

■ Teachers who would like new and practical ideas for their work, or some old ideas confirmed.

■ People just graduated from an education school who are about to start their new career.

■ Younger people, just out of college, who know their major subject well but who don't know much about teaching methods and don't want to start out by spending a couple of years getting an education degree or teacher certification.

■ The growing number of people who, having been in other careers, see our nation's special need for able, experienced people to teach and want to give it a try without going to education school but who need to know more about "how to teach" than they remember from how they were taught.

Eric W. Johnson
Winter 1987

1.
Order

When I asked 400 boys and girls in grades 5-9 in public and private schools "What are the most important qualities of a good teacher?" the ones they mentioned most often were, more or less in their own words, "Strict, firm, in control," "Interesting, makes learning fun," "Nice, kind, helpful, relates well to students," "Keeps a balance between control and freedom."

These qualities of good teaching—order, interest, spirit, discipline—are as inseparable from and dependent on one another as fire, water, air, and earth were to the ancients as the building materials of the universe. To clarify some matters and give workable suggestions for teaching, the first four chapters treat these elements one at a time, starting with order.

Order vs. chaos

In every school and in every classroom, order is better than chaos, even though there are times when permitted chaos can be extremely educational. While order for its own sake is a pale virtue, every classroom does need a backbone of order to hold up the marvelous body of learning, with all its organs and systems.

It is best to have a clear idea well before school starts what the backbone of order in your classroom is going to be and, with your students' help, to start building it the first day. It is far easier to relax a fair system of orderliness later on than it is to start with chaotic bits and bursts, even with the friendliest intentions, and then try to reassemble a workable skeleton of order that will permit learning to take place.

You have a big advantage the first day. If you don't use it, you may feel like the new third grade teacher who said, "Teaching is like trying to hold thirty-five corks under water all at once."

Order in upper grades

In upper grades, where the students usually come to you for only a single period, it is essential to have classroom routines clearly thought out in advance and to explain them early. Here are some suggestions, especially for the first day.

■ Write your full name on the board and let the students know how they are to address you—"Mr. Johnson," "Eric," "Sir," or whatever else the school's custom is. Don't try to be popular by asking them to call you by your first name when all the other teachers insist on being called "Mr.," "Miss," "Mrs.," or "Ms."

■ Tell students where they are to sit or let them know that they may sit wherever they wish.

■ When everyone is there, wait for the class to be quiet and then explain or tell whatever you have planned. Don't shout over a noisy class, except to say that it is time to start. Better than shouting is just looking ready to say something important that nobody wants to miss. If this doesn't work, a firm, friendly "Class!" will do.

■ Explain and carry out roll-taking procedures. Once you know your students' names, you can take the roll as they come in or just look early in the period to see who is absent. When meeting a class for the first time, let the students say their names so that you will know how to pronounce them; then say them back.

■ Learn everybody's name and preferred nickname, if any, even if it takes a while. One way to do this is to make a seating chart and mark individual students' names by their places, asking them to sit in the same places every day until you know all their names.

■ As soon as necessary, explain procedures for handing out materials and collecting papers and make them as simple as possible.

■ Have something on the board to engage the attention of all the students the minute they come into the room, headed "To do as soon as you are seated." Examples: "Write down 5-10 actions you observed between getting to school and now. Try to choose actions you think most people didn't see." "Look around the room and write down several ways you think it could be improved." "Estimate the number of printed books you can see in the room and divide by the number of students. How many books per student? Estimate what percentage of the books belong to students and what percentage belong in the classroom." It is always wise to have something ready for everyone to do in case you are delayed or have something you have to attend to before speaking to the entire class.

■ Explain that you expect people to raise their hands and be recognized by you before speaking so that each may be heard and all who want may have a turn. Stick firmly to this procedure unless or until you and the class agree to modify it.

■ If you are new to the school, find out from other teachers what the systems are, learn them, and apply them in a straightforward, friendly manner. Later, you may want to change things in your room, but early in the school year know what the established systems are and use them. You can be quite sure that most of the students will know them. If you and they are familiar with the school and its routines, the best way to begin the first period is to launch right into the subject of the class or course.

The best general approach to routines is a brief explanation that can be understood and followed. Always be open to reasonable questions about procedures, however, and be ready to change them if the change makes sense and doesn't go against established school practice.

Order deliberately challenged

Occasionally a student, or even a class, will start the year determined to test the teacher, especially a new one. Does he have authority? Can she manage things? Can we have some fun at the teacher's expense?

When students are bent on contest, you can avoid a lot of grief by making sure you win—not by putting them down or making them feel bad about themselves, or rubbing in your victory, but by seeing to it that the expectations of order, consideration, and teaching prevail over the will to disrupt.

How can you win? By explaining, without losing your cool, why you require whatever it may be. Don't call down the entire class; deal with one of the ringleaders, by name. Try to avoid being an adversary; let it be this student's behavior, as measured against commonsense expectations, that is the problem: "There's no way you can learn biology this year if you can't hear instructions," not "I won't have you talking while I'm trying to talk."

If you think it will work, back off from the one-to-one contest and say something like "OK, we're obviously not getting anywhere this way. What's the problem?" and let the class discuss it, speaking one at a time, with emphasis on what kinds of behavior will solve the problem. But don't let the discussion go on so long that it becomes a useless digression.

If these approaches don't work, use the authority of the school to re-establish order. First, warn a misbehaving student: "If you can't settle down so that we can go on, I'll have to send you to the office." Don't get trapped by saying, "The next person who says a word will be sent to the office," because sure as fate that next person will be a cooperative soul who is just trying to be helpful.

Then, if misbehavior continues, send the student from the classroom to a specific place and person, preferably with a note, and follow up afterwards by talking with the student and with the staff member to whom the student was sent. It is very important not just to send a student out of the room. Constructive action must follow to help develop behavior that works well for the student and for the school.

Finally, don't feel weak or ashamed about using others in the school — the principal, "the office" — to help maintain order in your classroom. Having done this once, you probably will not have to do it again, or at least not often.

Three contributions to order

A major contribution to order is for you as a teacher always to act as an adult. Students have plenty of other students to talk to but relatively few mature teachers. If you act your age, speak your age, and dress your age — but are friendly, open, and ready to listen and help — you are teaching students to deal realistically with their world outside school.

Yet another sort of order you can help promote is the order of truthfulness. You can expect your students to be truthful, but don't be blind to the fact that they sometimes are not, even if only to protect a friend. Never lie to a student. If you don't know the answer, say so; if you choose not to comment on a topic or situation, say so; but never make up an answer, and never deceive.

Third, you can let your classroom exemplify order. It should be kept clean, even if you have to clean it yourself, but it is better if you can persuade the students to help. Before long, when they do help, desk marking falls to near zero. After all, if the teacher doesn't care enough to keep the place clean, why should the students?

Order and very young children

It is perhaps even more important to establish a good base of order with very young children than with older ones. Most secondary school teachers, seeing the easy, happy, seemingly casual behavior of a well-run nursery school or kindergarten, do not fully appreciate the planning, thought, care, and expertise that go into making things run well and setting the stage for learning.

In some schools, the kindergarten teacher visits the children at home before school begins, sees their rooms, and takes the first step toward a friendly relationship. Often only half the group comes to school the first day, the other half the second day, so that the children may be given lots of individual attention as they enter the school, begin to learn how school works, and become willing to separate from the parents who may accompany them.

Procedures differ, but here is a typical one. The teacher greets the children one by one and takes them to their own place—a locker, cubby, or table and chair—where they can put their things, which they can call their very own, and on which their name is written along with a picture of an animal or some everyday object. The teacher then hangs a cardboard placard with their name and picture around their neck for all to see— *their* name. The children are given a quick individual tour of the premises, especially the bathroom, and are allowed to choose a quiet activity from the many available—blocks, crayons, scissors and paper, push toys—to keep busy until everyone has arrived.

5

Then comes an attention signal—a chord on the piano, lights flicked on and off—and, once everybody is quiet, the children are asked to assemble in a circle on the rug. Each child is asked to say his or her name, then to repeat it loudly and clearly. Everyone in the room, perhaps starting with the teacher, is invited to tell about anything they want to, but no one *has* to speak. Then the children can go on to some other activity, such as a song, game, or story that everyone will like—like even better than being at home.

After another free period, the attention signal is given for juice time and the routine is explained: "Please wash your hands, pick up your cup, pass by the pourer to get your juice, sit down and drink at any table you wish, get up and push your chair in when you've finished, drop your cup in the wastebasket, then go to the rug."

When nap time comes, the children are excused to go to the nap mats, one or a few at a time, by name or by categories (all with red socks, all with hair ribbons, all with belts), where they should stay, with a toy if they wish, but quietly if they do not want to sleep.

Since most nursery school and kindergarten children arrive with an attitude of awe rather than bumptiousness, the purpose of these routines, in the early days, is to establish a safe, consistent setting with reliable boundaries that makes the children feel comfortable, free, happy, and stimulated: "This is our place."

As time goes on, an understanding of certain rules gradually develops: be kind, be helpful, share, take turns, put away what you have taken out when you're done with it, throw things in the wastebasket, no pushing, no piling (unless it's a piling game), no running (except in the running place), no squashing, no shouting (unless it's a shouting game), no screaming indoors, no hitting other people (if you need to hit, go punch the punching balloon—a large plastic beanbag), no messing with other people's cubbies, and, if you need help, ask for it.

Order and rules

When we think of order, most of us think of rules. The best schools tend to have the fewest rules. But some students, especially in grades 4-10 or so, prefer to make up complicated systems of rules as a substitute for figuring out what to do about the various situations that arise.

However, figuring out and discussing what to do about problems of human relations are just about the most important part of education. Having too many rules stifles this kind of thinking. There are three things to remember about rules: rules should be few, needed, and written down; rules should be open for discussion and change; and rules should be obeyed until changed.

Some schools may need more rules, some fewer. Often rules are a suitable subject for discussion, writing, or group thought. All teachers should know and enforce the rules of the school, even though they may not agree with some of them. The only exception is in a teacher's own classroom, where some educational purpose might be served by not applying the rules.

It is all too easy to appreciate order for its own sake. To some, education is merely a matter of telling children how to behave and punishing them when they don't fit the mold; of preaching what to believe and having them say "We believe," or at least not hearing them object; and of filling their minds with knowledge only so that they may return it, verbatim and unconsidered, in a test paper.

In 1925, educator Agnes de Lima wrote *Our Enemy the Child* (New York: Arno Press), in which she castigated ordermongers: "On one thing only are they agreed—the child . . . must be subdued and transformed from the alien, independent being he was created, to a creature more pliant to their purposes. The theory of infant damnation still animates too much of our educational policy. Children must be cured of their original sin, have the nonsense knocked out of them, be molded into shape."

A more recent teacher, Kim Marshall, in *Law and Order in Grade 6-E* (Boston: Little, Brown, 1972), compares students in schools to "tidal pools near the ocean, in which a marvelous and colorful variety of marine life flourishes—crabs, underwater flowers, and so forth—when the water is calm. . . . The effect of the strict disciplinarian on kids [is] . . . similar to the effect of the incoming tide on these pools: the flowers close up tight, the crabs run into cracks and caves, and everything becomes still and colorless as the waves pound overhead." But Marshall would surely agree that students in our classrooms do need intelligent, understandable rules and order.

2.

Interest

The best sort of order in school is not the order imposed from above or by a sense of duty. It is the order that results from interest in subjects being studied and in the stimulation provided.

I was struck by this a few years ago in a Quaker meeting for worship as I looked out over a sea of 250 children in grades 2-6. They were well behaved but in a constant state of motion that reminded me of seaweed waving in the gentle currents of tropical waters. Moved to rise and speak, I told a story about nearly falling off a mountain. As the suspense grew, the motion ceased. Everyone gradually became still, intent on the story, until the suspense point passed; I didn't fall off the ledge. As I ended by drawing a brief lesson from the experience, the seaweed resumed its gentle movement. Thus interest creates order.

Further, truly good order is maintained by interest. Chapters 5 and 6 suggest some ways of teaching skills and subject matter that hold interest and result in learning. For now, here are a few general ideas.

■ If you are fortunate enough to have your own classroom, make it attractive and stimulating. The room should at least be clean and neat, without being too neat, and as well provided as you can manage with posters, pictures, books, maps, games, and other physical tools of learning. Another possibility is an absolutely clean, bare room on the first day of school, with lots of empty space on walls, shelves, and surfaces to be filled in the days to come. Nearly all students like to decorate and enliven their own room. No dull, bare room should sit unimproved for more than a few days.

■ Be convinced that whatever you teach matters to the lives, needs, and interests of your students. If it doesn't, change what you are teaching or change jobs. Your interest and conviction are contagious; so are your boredom and indecision.

■ Allow for digressions. Don't be so obsessed with the essentialness of every lesson and class period that you can't give way to something special and off the subject, like an all-day trip, an interesting unexpected visitor, or a burning concern that arises right in your class and causes a legitimate detour. In other words, be convinced of the importance of what you and the class are doing, but keep it in perspective.

■ Do your best to see that everyone in the class has enough to do and gets some feeling of reward and satisfaction from doing it.

■ Know, or learn as quickly as you can, your students' attention span and try not to exceed it. Attention differs for each student from day to day, from subject to subject, from activity to activity. By realizing this, you will come to know when force from the outside, rather than interest from within, is the main motivating force.

■ Always be ready for a change of pace if interest is flagging. It doesn't hurt to have a few games or contests in your repertoire, a joke or two, or even a couple of minutes of calisthenics.

Two kinds of motivation

There are two kinds of motivation: inherent and extraneous. Inherent motivation arises from interest and pleasure in the subject itself or from students' sense that what is being taught is important to them and their prosperity and survival in the world. Extraneous motivation works outside the matter being taught — the desire to stay out of trouble, to please the teacher, to get good marks, to meet the pressure of parents or peers.

It is unrealistic to expect inherent interest and pleasure to be a constant force. This is not necessarily bad, for the strong desire to get a good mark, if realized, results in a sense of achievement and perhaps enough learning to make the next steps more naturally interesting. And working to please the teacher, normally a rather low form of motivation, is better than no motivation at all. The important thing here is not to allow this motivation to become so connected to you that when you are gone all motivation is gone with you, and the student says, in effect, "Well, I learned math for Mrs. X because she's nice, but I sure won't do it for grouchy old Mr. Y." In general, if a high proportion of motivation for learning is extraneous, the learning is less likely to last and the motivation is more likely to shift to rebellion or to being turned off.

Relevance and interest

Try to teach, to show, to prove the relevance of everything you assign or require students to do. Explain, or, better, get them to explain through discussion, why the thing is worth learning. If you can't convince them, and if they can convince you that it is not worth learning, stop until you can figure a better reason or way to do it.

"Relevance" doesn't just mean something that will help students earn a living, even though that it legitimate. The eventual achievement of pleasure from Latin literature, after two years of suffering through grammar and Caesar, is relevant, if you can show it to be, but being able to read what it says on coins and knowing what *bis in die* means on a prescription is not. Meeting college requirements, getting on a varsity team, being popular, and being promoted to the next grade are relevant, if not the highest reasons for learning.

Be ingenious, persuasive, and constant in showing the relevance of what you teach. Be realistic, fair, and patient about the relevance of other legitimate claims on students' attention.

3.

Spirit

Without order, nothing much else is possible, but in the long run spirit is more important than order. Good spirit in a school arises partly from interest and partly from the way you as a teacher treat students and the way they treat one another. With good relations in the classroom, or in a class, almost any other good thing is possible.

Creating good spirit

How do you create good spirit? Let me suggest seven dos and seven don'ts.

1. *Be kind.* Through observation, intelligence, and empathy—and reading school files—try to figure out what each student needs and, to the best of your ability, provide it.

2. *Be polite.* Be courteous and considerate in your behavior and language, even when others are not polite to you.

3. *Let funny things happen.* Recognize and enjoy funny things when they happen. Sometimes it is hard to see the humor, but it may come to you later; you and the class can laugh about it tomorrow. If you and the class have trouble solving a problem, try to find something funny about it.

4. *Laugh.* Laugh *with* your students, or *at* a situation, but never *at* a student. Laughing together brings a group together, and the memory of laughing keeps it together.

5. *Let students be funny.* Some teachers, fearful of losing control, try to make themselves the principal source of humor. It is far better to let

students get a laugh from you and the class together; they feel better about themselves and about how they fit in, their spirits rise, and spirit improves.

6. *Respect each student.* If you show your respect for students, they will be more likely to respect themselves. Students who seem least lovable to teachers probably are difficult for others to love, too, and so they are most greatly in need of friendly attention. Even though all kinds of action and behavior cannot earn your respect, the *person* who acts and behaves, no matter how badly, must have your respect.

7. *Find something special to admire about each student.* Look hard, listen well, and find a chance to mention special things about students in public or in private, whichever seems better.

Now for the don'ts.

1. *Don't get angry at a person or a class.* If you must get angry, try to be angry at a situation or an action; anger toward a person is likely to beget more anger, close off communication, and ruin spirit. If you do get angry, have the grace to explain or apologize, which you can do without excusing the behavior that may have angered you.

2. *Don't scold.* Scolding finds fault and poisons spirit. It is an immoral luxury enjoyed by small-minded people in authority. Instead, state the problem briefly and get the class to discuss what can be done about it. (See Chapter 4, "Discipline.")

3. *Don't be cruel.* There is no excuse for inflicting pain and hardship for their own sake, which cruelty does.

4. *Don't embarrass students and make them uncomfortably self-conscious.* It rarely helps for a teacher to point out a student's individual faults, and never in public.

5. *Don't use sarcasm.* Wit is fine and humor a blessing, but sarcasm—wit used to show scorn or contempt—is just another form of cruelty.

6. *Don't make jokes about people's names.* It is best to play it straight on people's names. Even if a joke doesn't offend the person involved, chances are that the joke is stale.

7. *Don't invade a student's privacy.* Students may reveal private things about themselves, just as you as a teacher may talk about parts of your private life. What makes these exchanges acceptable, in private conver-

sation or in class discussion, is that they are voluntary. If you give even the appearance of prying, the barriers will go up.

Class meetings and spirit

Kim Marshall says, in *Law and Order in Grade 6-E,* that "most kids are not about to be remade." Most have basic self-respect and do not want anyone trying to change the basic self they respect.

Most classes are not about to be remade, either. They can remake themselves, and they can be helped to do it, but few teachers can say "Be and act this way" and get a class to do anything but obey the simplest rules. Individuals and groups need to feel that they control their own destiny and that they figure out how to improve their spirit and behavior.

They can still use some help, however, and one method is class meetings. Thousands of teachers over the years have used class meetings. Some problems that can be worked on in class meetings are fighting, bad language, unfriendliness, calling people names, bullying, treating people badly because of their race, not helping people who are lonely and friendless, bossing people, destroying property, playing hooky, being noisy and pushing in the halls, being cruel and persecuting people by teasing or hiding their book bags, stealing or messing with other people's property, making fun of people because of their clothes or personal habits, not getting homework done, not settling down when class begins, making a mess in the cafeteria, rushing to lunch tables to shut out unpopular people, feeling that schoolwork is dull and pointless, cheating and copying other people's work, feeling controlled too tightly—or not tightly enough—by the teacher, not having enough fun in school, not taking turns with scarce equipment, and feeling that the teacher has pets.

Almost any class or other school group exhibits some of these kinds of behavior or feelings from time to time. They are bound to have a bad effect on group spirit if they are not dealt with. The all-too-typical way for teachers to deal with these is to *tell*—to *tell* what the problem is, sometimes objectively, sometimes in a voice tinged with blame; to *tell* students how they should behave and how much better things would be if they did; to *tell* what the consequences will be if people don't behave properly.

13

This teacher-preacher-punisher system may work, at least for a time. It has the advantage of being simple, obvious, and easy to apply. But in most situations, especially those where the problem is serious and spirit is not so good, this doesn't work at all, or not for very long.

Why? Because it doesn't involve students in thinking or observing— only in listening and possibly obeying; it doesn't make anyone figure out possible solutions; it doesn't ask anything of the class except to avoid punishment by behaving in a teacher-prescribed way; and it may encourage students to evade or deny problems or to lie their way out of responsibility for behavior that doesn't work.

The class meeting method works quite differently. The class functions as a working group to solve problems by exchange of ideas. Class meeting discussions usually work best if the group moves into a circle, with the teacher, where it is easy for everyone to hear and see everyone else. The steps in the process are these.

1. *The class exposes the problem.* The teacher may start by posing a question: "I hear a lot of people complaining that there is too much messing around with other people's things. Is this just a lot of talk, or is it really a problem?" The teacher then presides over a discussion designed to bring out the facts. What is happening? Who is responsible? Is it widespread? Who is suffering? Any evidence is acceptable, but it must be evidence, not general blaming—and *never* name calling. If something is said that seems untrue—"Karen and Will are always messing in people's desks, and they take money"—the group is asked, "Is that true?" Although Karen and Will have a chance to deny it, they at least become aware that people think they are part of the problem, and so they may start to think about what they must do, or stop doing, to change what people think about them. Others may point out that it is not just Karen and Will, or that property was messed with when Karen and Will were not even around. It is always best to guide discussion toward reporting the facts rather than placing blame. The teacher should never blame and never judge.

2. *The class shows why the problem is serious for the group.* This phase may flow quite naturally from the discussion, or the teacher may start it by saying, "Let's move on and talk about whether the problem is really serious." Again, it is best to try to stay away from blame and to concen-

trate instead on how individuals and the group are being affected by the problem. Is it really harmful, or is it just people's imagination? If the class agrees that it is harmful, move on to the next step. But if discussion seems sufficient at this point, or the problem seems to have been solved, the teacher can suggest that this is so. If everyone agrees, they can get back to other school work.

3. *The class tries to figure out or devise solutions to the problem.* This process can have two phases. It starts with brainstorming. Students are asked to suggest any methods, practical or impractical, for solving the problem. The teacher notes these on the board as ideas to consider. When the brainstorming runs down, then the class looks at the board and considers, with the teacher, which suggestions might work. Those that will not are crossed off until, after discussion, all pretty much agree on a plan for solving the problem.

Up to this point, the class has been involved in thinking about its problems and figuring out solutions. This leads to habits of problem solving, develops communication skills, and turns people's energies toward acting better and not just retreating into hopelessness and blaming.

4. *The class commits itself to trying the agreed-upon solutions.* Now the meeting turns toward getting people to commit themselves to better ways of behaving by stating openly that they will try, by agreeing to take certain practical steps. The agreement can then be written out and posted on the bulletin board for a few days to remind people what they agreed on.

We all know that problems do not simply arise, get discussed, and get solved once and for ever by people committing themselves to today's solutions. Identifying and solving problems is a constant process, and class meetings are a constantly useful part of the process. They can keep students thinking about major problems and working to deal with them constructively. They develop the self-esteem, free communication, and sense of shared worthwhile objectives that foster good spirit.

4.

Discipline

Although "discipline" derives from the Latin *discere,* "to learn," in the minds of many people it has become synonymous with order and punishment. People seem to think that one of the worst things you can say about a teacher is that he or she is "not a good disciplinarian," and one of the greatest concerns about our schools is "lack of discipline." This means, I gather, disorderliness and bad behavior, which people believe result from the failure of schools to be strict, to make demands, and, when trouble breaks out, to punish. Of course, almost anyone who has ever taught school knows that things aren't nearly as simple as that.

One definition of discipline, according to the dictionary, is "systematic training in obedience to rules and authority, as in the armed forces." Such discipline may work in some schools and, during brief moments, in individual classrooms, but in the long run, as a steady school diet, such imposed discipline is not congenial to learning and does not develop character or maturity.

A second definition of discipline is "training of the mental, moral, and physical powers by instruction, control, and exercise." That is a broad, acceptable definition for us, especially if we are competent in our instruction, if we are able to arrange things so that the forces of "control" shift from outside the student to inside, and if we provide plenty of opportunity for the "exercise" — the use — of the student's powers.

Developing self-discipline

We will never know whether our students have developed any inner discipline, self-control, or independent motivation unless, occasionally

16

at least, we remove external controls and see what happens. One powerful element of external control is our conspicuous watching. Don't get me wrong: students need to be watched, and teachers who have developed, like P. G. Wodehouse's character Aunt Dahlia, "an eye that could open an oyster at twenty paces," possess a useful tool, much more effective and less distracting to others than a yell or a snarl.

Speaking of watching, I know a high school teacher, Emma, a tough, gentle, experienced professional, who told me that she had become expert in what she called the "overhead-backhand" method of writing. It enabled her to write on the board without ever taking her eye off the class. "It takes practice," Emma says, "but it is very useful. In schools like mine, to face away from the class for even a moment can mean disruption, ridicule, humiliation, and even personal injury"—a distorted Golden Rule applied: "Do unto others before they do unto you."

We must, however, be careful not to rely too much on the overhead-backhand technique, for an overwatched class never learns self-discipline. The key to helping students learn self-discipline, at least in a large, fairly traditional school, is to give them as much freedom to control and motivate themselves as they can use, and occasionally a little bit more. This means that we start with order and control, then put them on their own, bit by bit.

We measure out careful doses, starting by allowing the class to work independently on well-defined tasks while we work with individuals or small groups. We then encourage the class to devise routines for settling down and getting to work at the start of the period (or, easier, at the end) while we sit in the back. As a next step, we leave the class alone unexpectedly for a few minutes, arriving late on purpose to see what happens. Finally, we let individual students or small groups go to the library or work independently in the hall or in another room while we stay with the rest of the class.

These are only a few examples of allowed opportunities for students to "control and exercise" their "mental, moral, and physical powers" independent of our presence. In fact, in many an excellent classroom, students of all ages spend large portions of the day in self-controlled educational exercise of their powers.

The saying "We fail toward success" is often true of developing discipline in school. If we occasionally grant individual students or a class more freedom than they can manage successfully, temporary failure will result and discipline will break down. The breakdown of self-discipline can be the occasion for some excellent learning, provided the occasion is not used merely for preaching and punishing. By meeting—perhaps right away and just for a few minutes—exposing the problem, figuring out ways to do better next time, and then having the members of the class commit themselves to trying better ways, the class can strengthen its self-discipline.

I remember visiting one day an eighth grade classroom that exemplified the sort of attitude that helps develop self-discipline. At the front, the teacher had made a permanent sign above the blackboard: "It is safe to make a mistake in this classroom"—an excellent statement that, if applied, would encourage self-discipline and learning rather than merely timid attempts to avoid error. But the sign did not stop there. It continued, "but, more to your credit, to make a different one each time."

On the other hand, it is harmful for students, or anyone else, to be faced too often with challenges they are unable to meet. Teachers and students can learn the extent of their joint capacity to succeed. As someone has said, "Courage is the memory of past successes"; so are self-respect and self-discipline.

Discipline and "talking to" students

We need to try in every way possible to build self-respect and feelings of self-control in each student, for too many experiences in school end up with students feeling that they, as individuals, are failures. We tend to criticize and hold up and preach standards that our students are not yet able to meet. Then we correct and scold until they, feeling belittled, attacked, and devastated, become angry or withdraw and allow their emotions, not their brains, to direct their behavior.

I remember years ago seeing a cartoon in which one girl was saying to the other, "You know, the trouble with me is that I'm the sort of person my mother doesn't want me to associate with." It's funny, but it's tragic. An eight-year-old schoolboy in Rochester, New York, revealed the same sort of discouragement in his essay on "What My Dog Means to Me." He wrote, "My dog means somebody nice and quiet to be with. He does not say 'Do,' like my mother, or 'Don't,' like my father, or 'Stop,' like my big brother. My dog Spot and I just sit together quietly and I like him and he likes me."

We must support and respect our students, especially as individuals, as much as we can. That is quite different from supporting and respecting all their behavior. For example, a teacher asked Herb, a seventh grader, to be quiet in a study period. Instead, Herb ran out of the room and down the hall, with the teacher chasing him. As he zipped into another roomful of students quietly reading, the teacher caught him by the arm. After a dramatic silence, Herb shouted, "Help! Help! Reality's got me by the arm!" Reality then took him to a quiet place, and they talked over his behavior, but not his worth as a person, which, obviously, both he and the teacher respected.

One of the main opportunities we have to help students develop self-discipline and successful behavior is in our talks alone with them. What I am about to suggest is sensible, not very difficult, and it usually works. Some teachers have trouble with it because it goes contrary to their habits and to the way they remember being treated — scold-preach-punish, with the teacher doing most of the thinking and talking and the student mostly listening, resenting, and feeling put down.

The method works best in a private quiet session with the student, but it can also be used — briefly — right in a class when someone's behavior makes it necessary. It also works for guidance counselors and principals, and even for those poor souls called "disciplinarians." Students who are sent to the principal or other higher authority come back from the session feeling better about themselves and also behaving better.

The essential attitude the teacher and student must maintain, when following this method, is that the student's behavior, not the student as a person, is the problem. Always focus on the behavior and how it can be changed. Keep the atmosphere warm, friendly, and objective. Now for the specific steps.

1. *Ask, do not tell, the student what he or she is, or was, doing.* If you are warm and friendly, the student will tell you honestly, because you both know that help, not punishment, is your reason for talking together.

2. *Ask the student to decide whether his or her behavior is good or*

19

bad, helping or hindering. Is it helping the student, the student's class-mates, the school? Or, like Herb's disruption of study period, bad be-cause it bothers others? Being a confident, bright, and argumentative person, Herb would probably also say that he *likes* to talk, that it really doesn't bother anyone, that he doesn't mind when other people talk, and that study periods are stupid anyway. If he says this, you need to question him more deeply, especially about the effect of his behavior on himself, on others. Remember, you don't tell him; you ask him, and he thinks it out and tells you — himself. This kind of questioning provides important education in responsibility, or in acting on knowing the consequences of what you do, both for yourself and for others, now and later.

3. *Ask the student to figure out a better way of behaving,* one that will work better for the student and for everyone else. If, like Herb, the student has behaved this way for the twenty-sixth time, clearly the discus-sion needs to go deeper. If the student can't think of anything, you can help by making suggestions, in the form of questions: "Does where you sit have anything to do with the problem?" "Do you have any work or reading to do during study periods?"

4. *Ask the student to commit himself or herself to a better way of be-having,* even to the point of writing a statement of intention to do or stop doing what is needed. Stating an intention is better than making a prom-ise, because promises should not be broken, and you may feel bad or immoral if you don't keep a promise. An intention is only that — determination to do something, but without the moral overtone of a prom-ise. If you don't have the strength or will to carry out an intention, you don't need to feel that you are a moral failure, or no good as a person, but only that you aren't able to do what you honestly intended to do.

5. *Allow the consequences, good or bad, to happen. Accept no excuses if the student does not carry out a commitment.* This is very important. Too many of us are too busy, too indulgent, or too hopeful that if we let something pass just this once it won't happen again. Students should not be protected from the reasonable consequences of their failing behavior. If the student fails, start again with the first step until understanding, de-termination, and strength are developed.

A number of don'ts are connected with this method of developing self-discipline.

1. *Don't use students' pasts against them.* It is helpful, of course, for you to be aware of the past—that a student has displayed the same sort of failing behavior for several years—because almost certainly the student is also aware of it and feels weighed down by it. But never say anything like, "You've been acting this way ever since fourth grade. Aren't you ever going to stop?" That just generates a feeling of greater hopelessness. Instead, assume that right now is a new moment that offers a new beginning and a new chance for success.

2. *Don't preach or dictate.* Preaching or dictating stops students' brainwork; the point is to get students to figure out how to behave.

3. *Don't reject students.* No matter what, stay friendly and objective. You are not out to remake people; you are there to help them behave successfully.

4. *Don't accept excuses,* but do listen to explanations. This method works very well in dealing with serious kinds of failing behavior, such as stealing, cheating, not doing one's work, antagonizing other students or teachers, habitual fighting, refusing to answer in class, cutting classes, using drugs or alcohol in school, cutting other people down, and so on.

Discipline and punishment

Punishment is our traditional response to people's bad behavior: tell them it's bad, tell them to stop, and punish them for being bad.

I am always humbled, though, by a survey in which some nine- and ten-year olds were asked which they preferred when they misbehaved—a spanking or a friendly talk with the teacher. They voted overwhelmingly for the spanking. One can only suppose that they had had "friendly talks" before and knew that such talks took a long time, were boring, covered what they already knew, required sitting still and listening, and made you feel guilty and bad afterwards. Spankings had the advantages of being short, being clean, and making you feel that you had paid your debt, gotten what you deserved, and were free to go out and be yourself again, with few regrets.

But in my survey of 400 middle schoolers, when I asked, "Has anyone at home or school ever used corporal punishment (spanking, hitting) on you?" 46 per cent of the boys said yes, 54 per cent no, and with the girls it was 40 and 60 per cent. In response to "What were the effects on you?" 29 per cent said that in one way or another they were good, 70 per cent bad. Since nearly three quarters of the students said that the effects of corporal punishment were bad, I think we must give considerable weight to comments made by the opponents of corporal punishment: "It does not make as big an impression on me as talking," "I felt bad," "It made me a sad child," "It only hurts and builds grudges," "It does not explain what I did wrong or why," "It makes me say I didn't do what I *did* do, and that's a lie. Is that good?" and "I get madder and go out of the way to do bad things."

In the case of the talkative, confident Herb, one might ask, "Doesn't this kid know perfectly well what is wrong with his behavior? Doesn't he get a bang out of all the attention it brings him? Aren't there shorter ways of dealing with him and leaving more time for really serious matters?" Yes, of course; applying clean, no-nonsense punishment might do the trick. But if you are going to punish, here are some suggestions.

■ Never punish a failing child or student, except in the rare case where failure is due to pure laziness; only punish a basically confident, successful one who can take it in stride.

■ Never use a punishment that humiliates—like forcing a child to write or say that you were right and he or she was wrong—or any kind of public punishment, except for a brief, factual calldown—and even these can become a bad habit of teachers.

■ Never withhold your appreciation for the child, and never attack the child as a person.

■ Let the punishment fit the crime and, if possible, follow naturally from it. For example, logical punishment for cheating on a test is a no-credit mark, being assigned to study the material again, and being required to take another test. Relevant punishment for repeated talking in a quiet study period might be to sit at a desk away from everyone else.

■ Let students suggest their own punishment. If it is fair, suitable, and reasonable, use it.

■ Never punish students by requiring them to do more of something that is a vital part of their education, like writing an extra report, reading an extra book, or doing five more math problems. This only creates or strengthens an association between legitimate work and bad feelings.

■ Don't use silly punishments, like writing, "I will never . . . again" a hundred times.

Dealing with cheating and plagiarism

A special problem related to discipline and developing successful independence and self-respect is cheating. There is no question that cheating is fairly common in schools where conditions permit it and where there is any degree of competition or pressure. Some people argue that one way to end cheating is to take the academic pressure off students and to give up marks. There is little doubt that these steps would radically reduce cheating; after all, why cheat if there is no pressure and no marks? But eliminating pressure and marks does not teach honesty; it merely removes the motivation to cheat. The real challenge for schools is to teach honesty even when high performance is very important and when a reasonable amount of competition is present—two familiar parts of many segments of life.

When I asked the 400 students in grades 5-9 why they cheated (the cheating rate increased from 31 to 67 per cent from grade 5 to grade 9), they gave these reasons, arranged in descending order of frequency: "I want a good grade," "I forgot to study," "To get the answer," "It's a game, and when the person is not looking it's their fault," "When the answers are right under your nose and the problem is much too hard," "Everybody was doing it," "I'm scared if I flunk my parents will punish me," and "When I know how to do it and it gets boring."

Common sense, experience, and the replies quoted above show that cheating is likely to take place when one or more of the following conditions are present: seats are too close together; the work tested or assigned seems pointless or unreasonable; the work is hard and not well taught; there is tremendous emphasis on marks for their own sake; and students strongly dislike or do not respect the teacher.

Let me suggest some policies and practices that work well to decrease cheating.

■ Try to keep the work interesting and convince students that it is important to learn. Make it challenging but never beyond the capacity of most of the class.

■ Admit frankly before the first test of the year that cheating often occurs in schools and say that it is only sensible to move desks apart and cover answers that are easy to see. Without making students feel any distrust on your part, you will convey the idea that you know what's what.

■ Find an early opportunity for class discussion of reasons for cheating and its effects. This is also the time to talk about plagiarism—what it is, what it is not, and why it is a serious offense. (Before holding this discussion, be sure you know the school's policy on cheating and plagiarism.) It is surprising how many students have never thought much about these things.

■ Keep alert during tests and, when marking papers, watch for verbatim duplications. Don't be blindly trusting. That may reward dishonesty.

■ Take away the paper of any student who is clearly cheating, give it no credit for the test, and after class arrange a time to talk alone with the student. "Setting an example" by drastic, overt action is not only unnecessary but creates such bitterness and alarm that no lessons in honesty can be taught—or learned.

■ When you talk with the student, find out why he, or she, cheated and try to help her overcome the need for it. Get the student to explain, if possible, how cheating is self-defeating and how it may affect her reputation. But you must also explain that cheating is quite frequent and that this particular episode, while serious, does not put a permanent blot on the student's record, especially if it does not happen again.

■ Ask the student whether she would like to have you tell her parents or whether she would rather do it herself. Explain that parents need to know when their child is in trouble so that they may help. If a child is obviously afraid of her parents, and a surprising number of those who cheat are, you might let her off this one time without telling her parents. If she says she will talk to them, then check in a day or two and ask how they reacted.

No teachers—or parents, when they know about it—should let an incident of cheating or other dishonesty pass undealt with. If people get away with cheating, or stealing or lying, they are more likely to keep on doing it. In the long run, dealing promptly and incisively with cheating, and taking enough time to do it well, helps to prevent future incidents. More important, it saves the morale of the offender and the others involved. Honesty does not grow naturally; it is nurtured as teachers, students, and parents speak and act in situations where honesty is tested.

In schools where students are encouraged to work together to teach one another, it is important to teach children, especially in the early grades, that there are certain special times when you have to work alone and when sharing ideas and information is not permitted. Be sure that they understand, through discussion, the reasons for tests and the special way people have to behave during them.

The influence of a teacher's example

To the earlier definition of discipline as "training the mental, moral, and physical powers by instruction, control, and exercise" I should add one other means of developing discipline: the teacher's example. It is tiresome to be told that you have to exemplify all the qualities that you are expected to teach, but the better the example you set, the better your teaching of self-discipline will be. Here are six qualities that teachers need to keep in mind.

1. *Reliability.* Let your yea be yea and your nay be nay unless you are shown to be wrong, in which case admit it; don't hide it.

2. *Honesty.* Never lie or distort, if you can help it. Be honest about your errors, and your students are more likely to be honest about theirs.

3. *Promptness.* It takes no longer to read and mark homework and papers today than it will next week. If you know you can't get papers back promptly, say so and tell why. Otherwise, be just as punctual as you expect your students to be.

4. *Sensitivity.* Show that you are aware of how your class is feeling as a group and as individuals. Chapter 21, "Keeping in Touch," gives some suggestions on how to go about this.

5. *Self-control.* Show that you are in control of your powers—especially

your power of language — and use them reasonably. This means not talking self-righteously, not being sarcastic, not explaining more than students need to know to get on with their work. And, when the occasion arises, try to demonstrate how to control feelings by telling the class how certain kinds of behavior make you feel rather than by letting yourself be carried away by those feelings.

6. *Fairness.* There is practically nothing students resent more than unfairness or the appearance of unfairness. Never have a favorite, or if you do have a few — some students are certainly easier than others to like or enjoy — keep it a secret. Sometimes there are reasons for treating one student differently from another in the same circumstances, but the reasons should not be based on favoritism. You can tell classes you believe in fairness and are going to do your best to be fair but to admit that you aren't perfect and may slip unintentionally from time to time. Ask your students to tell you when they think you are being unfair so that you can either correct the injustice or explain why you did what you did.

Be sure, as you try to exemplify these qualities, that you do not seem to be saying, by your demeanor, "Look at me. How good I am." Just *be,* the best you can, and remember the little child's prayer: "Dear God, please make the bad people good and the good people nice."

The spectacular teachers — martinets who never missed when throwing an eraser, actors who imitated characters from history or dramatized events, or those who shared their personal lives, with emotion, and made us realize that teachers were human, too — these spectacular teachers are often the ones we remember as great. But the most memorable teachers are usually not the best ones. The best teachers put first the subjects and the skills they are teaching, and they themselves are happy to be in the background.

Do not, therefore, go into teaching to be memorable, but to develop enthusiasm for subjects and skills and living. The most memorable thing about you may be your enthusiasm for what you teach and for what your students learn.

5.

Teaching the Basics: Instruction

Having talked about the conditions necessary for learning, what about learning itself? How do children learn? How do we encourage students to learn what they need to learn in order to lead useful, satisfying lives?

First we need to dispel the widely held false notion that being taught is the same thing as learning. We can all think back to times when a teacher was putting on a fine verbal and physical show but no learning was taking place. Let's face it; most of the learning that occurs in our classrooms occurs not because of direct oral instruction but because of conditions we help to create that cause students to learn for themselves and from one another. Now and then the right words at the right moment, or a clear explanation, may cause a sudden surge of understanding, but not very often. Most of what we say at our students, mostly from the front of the room, may look fine to a passing supervisor, and it may even impress the students as being exactly what a teacher is supposed to do, but let's not fool ourselves. Many teachers talk too much. We need to learn when not to talk.

The acid test for a school is whether it succeeds in teaching the basics, especially the ones it is supposed to teach—which are, traditionally, reading, writing, and arithmetic, but which can better be expressed as the *four* R's: reading, writing, reckoning, and reasoning. If your school does not teach students to do these four to the best of their ability, and if it cannot show by objective measures that it is doing so, it had better reform itself, no matter how many other fine and noble things it is doing or claims to be doing. The trouble with such a simplistic statement, however, is that it encourages people to think that to teach the three or four R's you just put children in rooms in rows and *teach,* either by pouring or hammering in, and when you're tired of doing that you get out the workbooks.

What are the basics?

When speaking about the basics, it helps to divide them into three categories: basic skills, basic substance, and basic attitudes, with "basic" meaning "necessary to know in order to lead a productive, happy, satisfying life in our society, today and tomorrow." Here is my list.

1. *Basic skills.* To speak, to listen, to observe, to exchange (communicate), to read, to write, to figure and compute, to think logically, to organize, to plan, to persuade (to present or defend a point of view in a manner that is convincing), to deal with conflict, to set challenging goals, to find and use help, to judge when to try to solve a problem and when to try to live with it.

2. *Basic substance.* To know how the world and the universe work (the sciences—physics, chemistry, biology, nature study, mathematics, geography), to know how humankind works—in individuals and in our own culture, and in other cultures (psychology, anthropology, sociology), to know what humankind has done and thought (history, the arts, religion, literature, philosophy), to know how to stay healthy and what to do if you aren't, to be aware of what the important questions are: "What does what I am studying mean?" "What still needs to be discovered? By me? By humankind?"

3. *Basic attitudes.* To be interested and curious, to be persuadable, to respect oneself, to respect others, to respect knowledge, to feel a tension between what is and what should be, to feel responsible for one's own actions.

You may find that it helps to measure against these basics everything that you and your students do.

The coverage syndrome

One additional idea about the basics: too many teachers suffer from the "coverage syndrome," that is, if a given piece or area of subject matter has not been covered in the teacher's presence, it has not been covered by the student. We must not forget that there is life after school, and after our given class, just as there was before school and our class, and that minds will go on covering subjects without our aid. One of our main objectives as teachers should be to make ourselves unnecessary to our students' learning. In that sense, it is much less important to teach a given amount of a subject than it is to teach students to *do* the subject, and other subjects, eventually on their own. They should become their own teachers, able to learn what they want and need to learn.

Instruction

Instruction and discussion should rarely be separated in school; they are separated here only for simplicity's sake. (See Chapter 6, on discussion.) Even the sort of instruction that comes from reading an assignment should involve constant mental discussion with the book as the reader tries to master its content.

Out and out instruction does have its place, however. When a student or a group really wants to know an answer and needs it now, and when there is an answer and the teacher has it, often it is best to say, "All right, I'll explain," or "Here, let me show you," and to go ahead and explain or show. But if the main value to students comes from thinking out the answer or figuring out for themselves what to do, or if it does not come from asking the teacher but asking the class, then it is best for the teacher not to instruct or give an answer. Teaching is not answering; it is asking questions and providing the means to find answers. Besides, most questions worth asking are not the sort that can be answered yes or no.

Teachers should not, however, just preside over exchanges of ignorance. When misstatements of fact are made, they should be corrected, and when no one knows the facts, they should be pursued, preferably by a student. Sometimes a few minutes of organized information giving are called for, when interest is high and facts are needed to continue the discussion.

For example, if someone writes on the board, "Haveing eaten our lunch, the car wouldn't start," it is usually better for the class to examine the sentence, discover the errors, and correct them than for the teacher simply to correct them or call on the first person who shouts out. If in the process some further understanding can be developed about rules — generalizations that are true — so much the better. But if somebody says, "You don't need an apostrophe to understand 'wouldnt,'" that is not an error for correction; it is a conviction worth discussing, requiring the class to weigh the value of "correctness" as a matter of social and professional competence versus the apostrophe as a bother.

The class may discover that the truth, or understanding, is not something to be crammed into us but to be drawn out of us. The best teachers create and capitalize on opportunities to involve their classes in discussion of the philosophic and moral aspects of whatever subjects are being studied.

Most teachers are strongly biased toward books and reading as sources of instruction. Books, I feel, except for parts of science and art, are the very best teaching devices: they are simple to operate, easy to program to meet individual needs; they don't burn out, or break when dropped, or come unplugged; and they are comparatively cheap.

But teachers must remember that some — and sometimes most — students have difficulty with books and reading yet still are well able to learn. For them, instruction may consist of brief oral presentation, panel discussion, film, computer programs, drawing, arguing, touching and handling, trying something out in the lab, taking a trip or a walk, or having to explain something to somebody else.

Two other kinds of instruction are drill and tutoring, which could perhaps be called *coaching.* In such things as learning a foreign language, where hearing and repeating key phrases and sentences in proper order several times over with proper pronunciation are essential, or physical education, sports, and music, where repeated practice of exercises or complex bits of team play are necessary, supervised drill by a whole class, by small groups, or one on one is very important. Also, students often need a bit or a lot of individual tutoring or coaching in a skill or a bit of subject matter.

Instruction, then, should be many-dimensional and involve more than one sense. That is why every classroom should have plenty of chalkboard space, chalk, and erasers as well as bulletin boards and space for posters. When a new word comes up, it can be written on the board to be seen as well as heard without interrupting whatever else is going on. Chapter

14 gives some specific suggestions for various kinds of non-book instruction.

Instruction and sequence

In giving instruction in most classrooms and in most subjects, we must consider the sequence in which we present the elements of the material. We should not try to teach a skill or a concept before students know another one they need first in order to understand the one being taught.

For instance, you can't learn to multiply until you know how to add, to do algebra before arithmetic; you can't accurately observe the behavior of a snake or a mouse until you are free of fascination and fear; or you can't understand why the stars don't fall down unless you know a lot of other things first. Most important, you can't learn much of anything academic unless you know how to read — even though bright dyslexics can fool the teacher and themselves by guessing their way and piecing together oral and printed clues, which is not really reading.

A word of caution: the sequence principle does not apply to and should not be forced upon certain important areas of learning. For example, you can read before you are able to name the letters in words in proper order, or write a sentence before you know the parts of speech, or a paragraph before you know a sentence. Many crimes against learning are committed by forcing children who can write fluently to stop writing and go back to attacking the language piecemeal. The same holds true with drawing and painting.

Teachers need to keep trying to figure out what students need to learn before they can learn something else. They need to avoid the utter waste of trying to teach multiplication before addition or of making children learn to stay inside the lines while coloring before being allowed to express themselves in art.

Developmental sequence: thinking

Another kind of sequence has to do with whether or not a student has developed the ability to do abstract thinking. For years teachers have been aware simply from common-sense observation that some students can think abstractly and some cannot.

Swiss psychologist Jean Piaget (1896-1980), a gifted observer of boys' thought processes (he paid little attention to girls' thinking), especially their ability to think logically, noted that "intelligence," whatever that may be, does not increase at a steady rate but in spurts. Thus the conventional IQ score, based on a performance-age ratio, often is not an accurate measure of academic intelligence, let alone other kinds of intelligence, because people shift from one stage of thinking to a higher stage at different ages.

Piaget named four stages of development, the first of which he called the *sensorimotor period,* when children perceive the world directly through the physical senses. By about age two, they have learned that actions have physical consequences and that they and their environment are not one and the same.

The second stage, the *period of prelogical thought,* typically lasts from age two to age five. Children's thinking during this stage contains a sort of "magical" element, wherein they are unable to distinguish clearly between events and objects that are experienced and those that are imagined. Many children are still at this stage in nursery school and kindergarten.

During the third stage, the *period of concrete operations,* children learn to observe, count, organize, remember, and reorganize concrete objects and to do mental operations without losing the distinction between real and imaginary. This is a good stage for acquiring facts. It lasts until about age eleven or twelve, *if* the children involved are going to move on to the fourth stage. Many people never do.

When those who go on do enter the fourth stage, the *period of formal operations,* they begin to be able to deal with abstractions, to reason about the future, to understand and construct systems of thought, and to put forth theories and test them. This stage comes with adolescence, typically between the ages of eleven and fifteen or sixteen, though it may come much later, and, in a few people, earlier. But many people never learn to think abstractly, never reach the stage where they re-examine their world or the people in it or themselves. Teachers need to know this, because to require a person who has not reached the period of formal operations to think abstractly is to require the impossible.

Developmental sequence: moral reasoning

Another developmental sequence on the journey from childhood to adulthood is levels and stages of moral reasoning—the ability to think about right and wrong, truth and falsehood, good and bad, the ability to understand and obey rules, the ability to think out rules of one's own and hold to them.

The contemporary psychologist Lawrence Kohlberg, like Piaget basing his studies almost entirely on observations of the ways boys think, has identified the sequence of levels and stages they go through as they develop their power of moral reasoning—reasoning, not necessarily behavior. He has identified three levels and six stages, starting at about age four. (Before that age, Kohlberg says, children display no "moral" reasoning but simply know or feel that "what I want and like is good.") Then, at about age four, as they may enter nursery school, they reach the first of three major levels, the *preconventional level.* This is the level, or time, before the rules of group living or of society become a direct force upon children's lives. Of the two stages at this level, stage 1 consists simply of avoiding punishment: if I am frowned at, scolded, or hit, I don't do it; if I am smiled at, praised, or patted, I do it. Stage 1 children defer to superior power. Stage 2 is based on the fairness of sharing: I'll be nice to you because then you'll be nice to me; you do me a favor, I'll do you one.

The preconventional level lasts, at least among most middle-class American boys, through grade 4 or 5. Some people never go beyond this level, however, and many regress to it in times of stress, as in adolescence. Some, on the other hand, go beyond it earlier than grade 4 or 5.

The second major level of moral reasoning is the *conventional level,* during which children reason according to what they think society expects of them. This level has two stages. Stage 3 is "the way I am supposed to be" stage, when children want to be good girls or good boys. "Moral" is what receives approval and gets you liked. Stage 4 is the law and order stage, where people believe in fixed rules and respect authority. Theirs is the reasoning of the Ten Commandments, not the Golden Rule. Most people probably never go beyond this stage, even some very intelligent and successful ones who argue that there is no better way to arrange society. This second level is similar to Piaget's "period of concrete operations."

Those who enter the third major level of moral reasoning, the *postconventional level,* do so through questioning the accepted rules and conventions and working out for themselves moral principles based on their own convictions, not on what someone else has told them is right. (They have reached Piaget's "period of formal operations," when they have developed the ability to think in abstract generalizations.) Kohlberg divides stage 5 into two parts. Stage 5a consists of agreements and obligations freely entered into and faithfully held. The writers of the United States Constitution seem to have operated at this stage of moral reasoning. (Obviously, teaching and reading and discussion would help a person move from stage 4 to stage 5.) Stage 5b is a morality based on individual conscience, an inner sense of right and wrong, even though the actions it dictates sometimes may go against or beyond what is considered the welfare of the community or the rules of society. Kohlberg says that stage 6 of morality, seen only in rare individuals, is based on "belief in the sacredness of human life as representing a universal human value" and deep commitment to that belief. Such figures as Buddha, Jesus, Hillel, Gandhi, and Martin Luther King come to mind as representing this highest stage of morality. Doubtless there are others, too, most of them living out their lives without ever becoming famous.

Piaget, Kohlberg, and adolescence

Moving into Piaget's formal operations period and Kohlberg's postconventional stage is likely to come with the passage through adolescence. "Adolescent" thinkers are those who, finding old barriers tottering, have to rebuild, to think anew, to find themselves again, to establish new relationships with all aspects of their world, including the physical and mental world within.

This process makes waves, a rough passage — much rougher for some than for others. The breakdown of the desire to look like a good boy or girl and of the established order of rules and respect causes stress. We all know that under stress we often regress to more childish behavior. So early adolescents, under the stress of the rough passage, may seem to regress to earlier stages of moral reasoning, a sort of relapse into what appears to be stage 2 — "sticking up for each other" — but only for a while, a sort of backsliding needed for a move forward to new levels of maturity.

We need to keep developmental stages of thinking and moral reasoning in mind, or at least the concept of growth in stages, if we are to fit our instruction to the various conditions of our students. It is especially important to understand that discussion, rather than up-front, teacher-dominated instruction, best helps students to move through to higher stages.

Also, we should not assume that typical third or fourth graders, not to mention kindergartners, are capable of thinking in generalities. If we teach directly for this, or if we give assignments and tests that require general thinking, we are probably teaching in vain, and we may even be slowing down the learning process by asking minds to do what they are not yet developed enough to do. So watch for the ability to think abstractly and be sure that the general truths or propositions that are arrived at are not solely those in your adult teacher's mind, or not a mere reciting without understanding of a general principle that you have written on the board.

The thinking of boys and girls

As I have said, Piaget and Kohlberg based their studies primarily on the reasoning and thinking of boys. In a way that is now hard to understand, they seemed to see girls as a sort of foreign land, or to forget that females, part of humanity, are not to be relegated to footnotes and considered as exceptions to the proper mainstream development of "mankind."

More recent studies, especially those of Carol Gilligan, author of *In a Different Voice: Perspectives on the Moral Development of Women* (Cambridge, Mass.: Harvard University Press, 1982), have shown that two "moral voices" speak when human beings are asked to make moral decisions, "to reason morally." One voice speaks of concepts of justice and rights, with rules that can be applied to govern and to judge human behavior. The other voice is more concerned with caring, with considering the effects on people of what is done, with responsibility for the consequences of our actions.

The first "moral voice" might be labeled *the ethic of justice;* the second, *the ethic of caring.* Gilligan does not say that the ethic-of-caring voice is better or worse than the ethic-of-justice voice, but rather that there are two voices and that both are important and must be heard and considered. In our society, and perhaps especially in our schools, the ethic of justice has been recognized, honored, and rewarded, whereas the ethic of caring—so much more complex and so much more difficult to express as a gradable decision that has been "mastered"—has been denigrated, even unheard.

We need to listen to both voices as we conduct class discussions, make reading assignments, make up tests, and grade students' performance. It helps to remember what Gilligan and others have found: that boys and men tend to think and act in terms of rules and "justice," whereas girls and women tend to think and act in terms of human relations and caring. Boys tend to decide more readily than girls what is the right thing to do in a given situation, or what is the definite answer to a complex question in history or literature. This does not mean that boys are more intelligent than girls, or less intelligent, but that their intelligences tend to work differently.

Dealing fairly with ethics of justice and caring

From a teacher's point of view, it is much easier to deal with ethic-of-justice thinking in class than it is with ethic-of-caring thinking. We tend to ask a question, call on one of the first few students who raise their hands, and give reinforcing approval to plain, clear answers. This works to the disadvantage of those students—most often girls but sometimes also boys—who are pondering our question more deeply and don't feel ready to plunge at once into a plain right-or-wrong, yes-or-no answer. For example, because of an experience in class or in the community, or an incident in a short story, or a piece of scientific data collecting, you might ask, "Well, is it ever OK to tell a lie?" Or in discussing discipline at school a question might be, "Should students be punished for being late to class?" Or around Christmas someone might ask, "Is it good for kids to believe in Santa Claus?" The masculine type of thinkers will be ready with a plain, probably vigorous answer, and the teacher will probably be pleased. The feminine type of thinkers will be pondering more deeply and asking themselves other questions, like "What would the consequences be?" "Doesn't it depend on what person you're talking about?" "How will people feel?" or "*Why* are people late?" or "It all depends on . . ."

Since boys tend to be encouraged to answer and to argue their points of view with definiteness and vigor, teachers tend to call on them more, praise them more, and approve of their independence. We must be sure that we do not unfairly encourage the quick, convinced, categorizable answer and discourage the thoughtful, deeper, possibly more caring answer. If someone says, "No, it's wrong to lie. It's obvious," we can ask, after a pause and after looking around the room, "Anything else to say?" or "Well, why do some people who seem to be good and kind sometimes not tell the truth?"

Chapter 6 gives more suggestions about conducting discussions. For now, if some students find it difficult to arrive at *the* answer that we tend to look for, we need to be sure that we do not attribute that difficulty to low intelligence or to inability to write and speak "plain English, in a straightforward way." As Oscar Wilde said, when asked for the "pure and simple truth" about something, "The truth is rarely pure and never simple."

Instruction and reading

Before talking more about discussion, I should say a word about the most vital skill: reading. Although I don't know enough to explain how to teach reading to beginners, for that is a special skill, I have seen enough good and bad teaching of reading in elementary school classrooms to be convinced that in most schools less time should probably be spent on "learning to read" and more time on reading to learn, reading to solve problems, and reading to enjoy. Beware of the approach that breaks reading up into 289 basic, particular skills to be learned, skill by skill, by way of worksheets, until the children become really expert at the dull tasks of checking the correct blank but never have time to read and enjoy an actual book. If they do read an actual book, it is a basal reader, with vocabulary and sentence length carefully controlled by level of difficulty. Most basal readers offer little joy or reward, and certainly no literature.

Instead, try to remember the following points about teaching reading.

■ Don't require students to be able to say letter sounds before they are allowed to read books.

■ Some children do require instruction in phonics, either systematic or, better, as the need arises when a word comes along that needs to be decoded. Provide these children with the needed decoding instruction.

But other children learn the decoding of symbols into sounds simply by reading easy, interesting books, by being read to aloud while they follow along, and by unconsciously learning the decoding rules as they proceed.

■ We may be thankful that teachers have not yet got hold of teaching very young children to speak, an even more complex task than learning to read. All children learn to speak by needing to speak, by getting constant positive and negative reinforcement from speaking, and by being surrounded by others who speak.

■ If you can manage it, provide a rich reading environment in your classroom—a wide choice of books, easy and hard, on many subjects. Try to get some money for a classroom library. Invite children to donate to the classroom books they have enjoyed so that, even without money, a library can be built up.

■ Use the school library frequently and be in contact with the librarians, alerting them to provide the books, or suggest some books, that the children will enjoy. If possible, arrange for a collection of books from the library to be transferred for a time to your room to make it easier for students to browse and borrow them.

■ Don't separate reading from all the other materials students are studying. Encourage and strengthen reading in science, social studies, art, and all subjects, and *never* separate "literature" from "reading."

Different kinds of reading

Even after children have learned how to translate printed and written letters into speech and then into ideas, they need to learn that there are several kind of reading and how to use them. Too many students, and probably most adults, believe that there is only one way to read, one that is far too slow and plodding for most material and yet not slow and careful enough for some other kinds of material.

Teachers should therefore be alert for opportunities to demonstrate that there are at least five types of reading and that the nature of an assignment or material should determine the type to be used. Here they are.

1. *Skimming,* for an overview of the material or to find specific items of information.

2. *Rapid, relaxed reading,* to enjoy a story or something that interests you.

3. *Close, active reading,* for mastery, used with textbooks, encyclopedias, and other materials containing facts and main ideas.

4. *Word-for-word reading,* perhaps aloud, for directions or for mathematics and science problems.

5. *Poetry reading,* best done aloud, for meaning, metaphor, feeling, and sound.

In giving students an assignment, take time to discuss with them what type of reading they think they should use and to show them, if need be, how the types of reading differ.

One special kind of reading that can be used to good and bad effect in the classroom is reading aloud. Perhaps you feel that students are helped if they get a feel for the rhythm and sound of a particular writer's work. If so, prepare yourself to read very well a passage or two aloud – usually much better than just assigning work to be read at home without any clues to its difficulties and delights.

Never require students to read aloud to the entire class unless you know they do it well. Even though you can often tell quite a lot about the state of students' reading by hearing them read aloud, some students find oral reading a difficult and embarrassing task. This is especially true if the rest of the class laughs at errors, because some errors are really funny, but not to the reader who is making them. Furthermore, being able to read aloud is no proof of a person's ability to read silently, or vice versa.

Giving directions

As a rule, teachers give directions too fast and not clearly enough for students who don't understand and too slowly for those who grasp them quickly. You can save confusion by working out in in advance how you are going to give directions. Here are some pointers.

■ Make directions clear and present them in steps. As you go from point to point, write each one on the board, in full or abbreviated form. Leave the written directions on the board so that people can refer to them later.

■ After each point, or at the end, ask, "Is that clear?" If it isn't, explain again in a different way. Do not repeat unless it is necessary. Teachers tend to repeat so much that students learn not to look or listen the first time.

■ When you are quite sure that most people know what to do, say that you will explain further at the end of the period, if people need you to, and leave time to do so.

■ If the assignment extends beyond one day, you can ask again, the second day, whether anyone is having problems with it. Don't go over it all again; just explain the parts that aren't clear.

■ Work out as many routines as possible so that after the first few days you don't need to give directions on such things as the form of papers, where to hand them in, what to do about a late paper, and when and where to get individual help.

What is a mind?

A mind, any mind, either rejects or processes what is poured at it— not into it. What gets in is argued with, reacted to, distorted, trivialized, glorified, hated, loved, mastered, or soon forgotten.

I like Plutarch's metaphor for the mind: "The mind cannot be seen as a pitcher that needs to be filled but rather as a flame that must be kindled and fueled." We should provide more kindling and rekindling, and we should open up the sources of fuel so that minds may burn on their own. But even Plutarch's metaphor doesn't work, because the kindled mind does not burn up the fuel, but illuminates and increases it, more like an atomic reaction.

Perhaps we ought to stop trying to find metaphors and use a careful definition, like this one: a mind is "the element or complex of elements in an individual that feels, perceives, thinks, wills, and especially reasons."

6.

Teaching the Basics: Discussion and Mastery

The best way to use much of classroom time is in group discussion, which is about the only kind of learning that can't be done just as well or better somewhere else.

First, let's be clear what discussion is not. It is not reciting memorized facts, and it is not coaching for mastery of certain material. And discussion is not the class trying to guess an answer that is hidden in the teacher's mind—a rather low form of activity, and dull to boot.

Genuine discussion occurs when questions that do not have a yes or no answer are put to the class and the teacher steps back to let thinking and exchange of ideas and opinions take place. Because the number of questions for discussion is infinite, you should have little trouble formulating some that grow naturally out of the subject the class is studying. Including such questions should be an important element in planning a lesson, a class period, or a week of work.

Conditions for discussion

If we are going to have good class discussions, we must overcome our fear of silence, especially since some of the most educational time spent in the classroom is spent in the silence of thinking as part of discussion—the "wait time" between question and attempt to answer. Too many of us, when we encounter a question to which there is no ready answer, shortcut the educational process by calling on the first hand raised or accepting the first blurt.

When a significant question is before an attentive class—"Is violence ever the best way to settle a problem?" "How can fiction be truer than nonfiction?" "Can calculators and computers help you be a better mathematician?"—then come the moments of intense education, unless the intensity is sprung by a quick answer or, worse, by the teacher giving *an* answer that is taken as *the* answer. It is far better to put the question and wait—ten, even fifteen, seconds, a long time in most classrooms, but a thin slice of the school day—until several hands are up, with everybody thinking, and then to call on one person to speak. Those post-question silences are the best but the rarest in schools.

To have this kind of discussion, you need to make sure the class understands that ordinarily no one is to speak without raising a hand and being recognized. Letting people speak as soon as they have a thought interrupts the others and allows fast or intuitive thinkers and confident talkers to dominate the discussion. Those who think more slowly or systematically may have ideas, too. Spirited conversation among the teacher and the four or five quickest students should not be confused with genuine class discussion.

In presiding over a discussion, you should be able to turn a question back to the class instead of giving the answer, which teachers so often do, and which classes so often expect them to do. For example, if in talking about having to raise hands a student says, "But I don't see why we can't speak when we have an idea. If we can't, it makes it so stiff," you can, without explaining why, just say, "Well, why not?" and, after that, "Does it really make things stiff?" and let the answers arise from the class.

Techniques and arrangements

Here are several suggestions for conducting a class discussion.

■ Don't repeat a student's comment. Paraphrasing or restating what a student has said so that everyone will be sure to hear and understand it is a harmful practice. It says to students that they don't need to speak up for anybody but the teacher, who is the source of all truth.

■ Don't dominate the discussion. Your function in a discussion is to preside over an exchange of ideas and opinions and to keep students talking with students. Whatever questions you ask should be for the purpose of keeping the group on the track and thinking with greater clarity. The art is in asking questions, or getting students to ask questions, that move the class toward resolving the issue being discussed. One exception to not making comments arises when a timid student finally says something and everyone ignores it, out of habit. Here's a chance to build the student up a bit, not just by saying "Good, Jamie," but by taking Jamie's idea and showing its worth by adding an example or stating another dimension of it, perhaps ending with a question: "What else can you think of that shows the importance of Jamie's point?"

■ Don't always call on the first student whose hand goes up. Allow time for several hands to go up. Perhaps you will call on the last one up, that of the less bold contributor who needs encouragement, or the one who arrives at the talking point more slowly than the others.

■ If possible, arrange the desks in a circle or a U. It is difficult to have an all-class discussion if the students can't see anybody's face but the teacher's without turning around.

■ When a student is talking, move away, not closer. If you move about the class during a discussion, it makes the student's voice carry across more of the entire group. (It is usually better to stay seated with the others.) And avoid exchanges with and between individual students, which tend to be inaudible to the rest of the class.

■ Always ask a question before naming someone to answer it. "What are some advantages of having opposable thumbs. . . [pause], John?" not "John, what are. . .?" The first way makes everyone think about the question, not just John.

■ Never call on students in any predictable order; that will guarantee a low percentage of involvement.

■ Keep track of who has spoken and who has not. If some students have not taken part at all during the period, or for several periods, look for ways to involve them, perhaps by calling on them even if they don't raise their hands but you think they may have something to say. You might even think up an "easy" question to ask and then call on the quiet people or ask them each to report on a familiar and relevant experience. But never invade students' privacy. All students have a right to be silent, and teachers have no right to insist that they relate all their experiences. We do, however, have a right, perhaps a duty, to put some pressure on them to answer questions on material they have been assigned to answer. That can be motivation for future effort, but it's not really discussion. It's recitation, which has its values.

■ Allow an occasional outburst of comment or reaction. If some non-recognized student makes a statement that stimulates almost everyone to talk and you find that the class has become a noisy jumble of excited comments, let it happen for a few moments. Real communication and exchange often occur at such times. After the buzz has died down, say something like, "Well, Mary, that really got a reaction. Josh, will you restate what Mary said? [Josh does.] Now, let's discuss it. Any hands?"

■ Small-group discussions are often better than all-class ones. If you have twenty-five students or more in your class, it is hard to maintain interest and general participation in a discussion. Breaking the class into small groups of five or six works well and gives everyone a much better chance to participate. Each small group needs a discussion leader. You have to be able to move the chairs so that the groups can cluster around the room; and it is a good idea to write the discussion question on the board so that the groups may refer to it. It also helps to give the groups "tasks" to accomplish: (1) "Be ready to report on one or two ideas that the group has agreed on," (2) "Be ready to state several interesting facts or experiences that relate to the subject," or (3) "Restate and report on the two or three most interesting opinions that came up." The group leaders should be ready to speak for their groups right after the discussion ends. A summary of the discussion—which is almost always dull and trite—is not called for.

Try to make the questions discussed by the class appropriate to their age. A class of first graders cannot meaningfully discuss "What are the advantages and disadvantages of democracy?" or "Is there any difference between brightness and wisdom?" but these might be excellent questions for students in grades 8-12. A sentence from a reader, maybe arising from a story or a fairytale, might let you ask, "Why did Alberta wear a blue hat?" or "How do people decide whether or not to wear hats and what kinds to wear?" or "Gabe got punished for what he did [in the story]. How did the punishment affect him?" and then, "What do you think about punishment? What is it? When should people be punished? How should they be punished?"

Some questions that kindergartners and the lower grades can discuss with profit and learning: "What do you think about crying?" "How could we make this room look better?" "What may happen soon to Mary's building-block house? How could she fix it?" "Is it ever OK to tell a lie?" "What do members of this kindergarten do especially well?"

Some subjects are not suited to the kinds of discussion being suggested — such as mathematics, foreign language, and some science instruction. In those subjects, large amounts of up-front, everyone-face-the-teacher speaking and demonstration are required. Boardwork that everyone can see is necessary. A correct answer, or correct pronunciation and word order, are essential.

Some benefits of discussion

From solid discussions come important benefits that constitute learning or developing many of the basics given in Chapter 5. People develop the skill and habit of listening. They learn to express themselves and to stand up for their ideas better and with greater confidence. The class learns to do a better job of exchanging ideas and communicating. People learn to let their minds be opened and changed as they hear and take in new ideas

Further, discussion trains students to question and seek answers and not to accept unthinkingly as truth statements and assertions made by others — a skill especially necessary for citizens in a democracy. Discussion can reveal aspects, dimensions, and possibilities of an assignment that are less likely to emerge if it is merely explained by the teacher.

Finally, discussion shows the teacher and the class how people are thinking and feeling, what interests them, and the ideas and experience they have.

Mastery of fundamentals

Some schools pass students from grade to grade without ever giving them the opportunity, much less requiring them, to master the skills they need to go on successfully. Consequently, many students fall farther and farther behind and get more and more bored with school until they drop out or, if resources and motivation are present, they are given strenuous, expensive remedial work to catch them up.

Those students who are not mastering the fundamentals are the ones who should have the first-priority attention of teachers. In the long run, this saves everyone time and trouble and makes more time for "creative" work as the gap closes between those who have mastered and those who have not. The following four steps help in teaching for mastery.

1. *Presentation of material.* Presentation should consist of a variety of methods and materials, not just teacher talk and assignments in books. After all, not everyone learns best by listening and reading.

2. *Participation and evaluation.* Students need to practice what they are learning. As they learn, most students—especially young ones and timid ones—need something that tells them how they are doing: a word of praise, a high score, a job obviously completed and mastered, even a gold star or a line going up on a progress chart, or the chance to explain to others, to help and be helped as the effort to learn is shared. At this stage, marks—many marks—can be helpful. Marks, or grades, properly used, give accurate information, a quick measure of success or lack of it, a sense of accomplishment, an understanding of where you stand in relation to mastering the subject and what you need to do next. (See Chapter 19 for a fuller discussion of marks.) The least confident, least competent students need the most participation and evaluation of their performance. In most schools, they get the least.

3. *Testing.* Here we are speaking of real tests, not the kind of testing involved in the previous step. A test may be a well-devised assignment or a set of questions that students tackle alone, with supervision, that show whether or not they have mastered the fundamentals (see Chapters 16-18).

4. *Further teaching.* Too many teachers stop with the third step. They record a grade and hand back the test, showing whether the student has mastered the material. That being that, the class moves on to the next phase of the subject. But that should not be that. Instead, primary attention should be given to those who have failed to master the essentials. This should involve several activities: reteaching, allowing those who know the material to help those who don't, working out fresh ways to explain, assigning new reading, experiments, and exercises, giving special help

in small groups and to individuals, and testing again when you think most of those who failed now know the material.

It is important not to punish those who haven't mastered the material. It is also important not just to repeat the same teaching process that failed to result in learning the first time.

One example of how to deal with failure I found in a most unlikely place, Temple Medical School, in Philadelphia, where one of my children was studying. Because one essential for practicing medicine is a thorough knowledge of anatomy, much of the first year is taken up with its study. After each major anatomy test, the 10 to 15 per cent of the class who fail the test are given a special privilege: the hottest-shot professor of anatomy holds special sessions for this group, dissecting a cadaver and brilliantly explaining as he goes along everything that they may not have understood when they were dissecting their cadavers. The class is closed; only those who failed the test, a small enough group to make real question-and-answer teaching possible, are allowed to attend. Afterwards, most of them pass the test. They have learned the fundamentals, and they are ready to proceed. This is a superb example of coaching.

What does the teacher do with those who have mastered the material when so much special attention is needed by those who haven't? More able students can work on individual projects; students can be grouped so that some parts of the work are still done by everyone together and other parts are assigned to individuals or groups; and homework assignments can be made broad enough to have the amount of time they take depend on the interest, ability, and time the individual student has.

This all sounds much simpler than it really is; later chapters discuss some practical methods. The simplest thing, of course, is to give everybody the same work and to teach everybody the same thing in class. The better way can be managed, however, and even by ordinary people who aren't geniuses or chained to their jobs.

A fine example of a teaching device to promote mastery is a rule I saw posted in a science classroom: "When in doubt, *think*. If still in doubt, *ask!*"

7.

Dealing with Written Work

Just as learning to read and to enjoy reading should be a part of all subjects, not just English, so should writing. Why learn to write well? This question is a good one to discuss with students from time to time.

Here are some benefits of knowing how to write well that students may bring out. Writing enables you to explain, give instructions; to persuade people to act or not to act; to convince, to sell yourself, your product, your service; to delight others and share enjoyment; to delight yourself; to make people laugh, cry, respond; to clarify your own thinking, especially when making plans or important decisions; to express your feelings to yourself, to others; to state questions that need answering; to keep records; to fill out forms; to communicate through letters; to earn a living; to thank people; to obtain things that you or others need; even to help society work better.

Correcting and editing papers

In most schools, teachers each have their own system of editing or "correcting" written work, and pupils need to learn the different systems, teacher by teacher, year by year. It makes more sense for a school to have a common set of symbols and a single system. It doesn't matter exactly what the system is as long as it is sensible, is not beyond the easy comprehension of students, and has some relation to symbols commonly used in the great outside world of writing.

When you hand back papers, students should work on revising them in the light of your corrections and comments. Some parts may need to be rewritten, but complete recopying should never be required unless a paper is sloppy. Insisting on perfect neatness stifles motivation. As long as revisions are clear and intelligible, you should accept them.

Some ways of going about correcting and editing papers work better than others. Here they are.

■ Don't swamp a paper with so many correction that it looks more like a disease than a piece of edited writing. "Correct" and comment on only as much as you think the student can deal with and not be discouraged. This may mean letting some errors pass, at least for the time being.

■ Don't be so preoccupied with simple mechanical errors, which you can learn to correct quite easily, that you do not give attention to larger and more important matters—mainly content, but also word choice, organization, and tone.

■ On any paper that represents more effort than a mere routine exercise, try to make an encouraging comment or two, if you honestly can, as well as suggestions for improvement, if necessary. Be sure students feel that their paper has been read and reacted to. Also, if there are some especially good bits, note those: "Interesting idea!" "Good word!" This motivates students to keep on writing, with pleasure.

Evaluating student writing

It is helpful to give all important papers at least three marks: one for *content* (what the paper says; by far the most important mark), one for *spelling* (the least important, except for the prejudice our society has in favor of correct spelling and people's mistaken belief that spelling and intelligence correlate), and one for *mechanics* (capitalization, punctuation, and indications of organization—paragraphing, etc.). These three aspects of writing are quite, though not entirely, discrete and thus should be marked separately.

If a student looks at a paper and sees "Content = B+, Spelling = C−, Mechanics = A" and then says, "Yes, but what did the paper *get?*" you can say, "It got three grades that should give you some useful information about your writing." Then you might add, "If you read the comment I wrote at the top and all of the editings and corrections in the margins, you will have learned something valuable about how well you write and about how to write better. Now, how about working on your paper some more?"

Persuading students to revise and correct

The best motivation is persuasion backed by requirement. When you hand back a batch of papers, you might make the following remarks, or something like them.

> When I give your paper back, you will probably need to revise it, to "correct" it, because writing should be a *process of improvement,* not setting down a fixed thing, getting it marked, and then going on to the next thing. It's like practicing a sport. If a move or a play goes wrong, the coach says, "That's wrong. Here's how you should have done it," and then tells the players to go over it again so that they learn to *do it right.*
>
> When you write a paper, you usually make some errors in spelling, punctuation, capitalization, and sentence structure, no matter how carefully you have gone over it. In most cases, I have suggested changes, perhaps in sequence and organization, development of ideas, need to strengthen the argument, clear up fuzzy ideas, or eliminate unnecessary repetition. You can benefit from these corrections and suggestions; they are directed specifically at you. Please revise your paper and make all the corrections; in other words, "Do it right." Very often, people learn more from revising a paper than from writing it in the first place.

Better than a speech is a discussion in which the class figures out for itself the benefits of correcting and revising papers.

A system for correcting and revising papers

Require students to correct and revise their papers after you have marked and commented on them, and let them know that revision and correction count in their final grade. Here is a system that works.

- Explain why papers must be corrected.
- Require that papers be revised and corrected and handed in the next day or, if much other work is being done, by another early time. (Much more learning takes place when things are fresh in people's minds.)

■ Require that every correction signal and suggestion for revision you have made be dealt with and the paper returned to you for rechecking. Keep up this exchange until you have given the paper final approval.

■ Mark the corrections and revisions, perhaps thus: OK = job completed, file the paper; + = good job, but some items still need to be dealt with; 0 = fair job, more to be done; − = poor job, more to be done. Keep a record of these marks in your gradebook.

This may seem like a lengthy, complicated system, but once it is learned and becomes routine, it is a quick and effective way to help students improve their writing.

Some shortcuts

No matter how fast, bright, expert, and decisive you may be, if you have five classes a day and 100 pupils or more and are having students write more than once every two weeks or so, you are going to have to use some shortcuts. They may not be the ideal way to deal with writing, but they are much better than nothing at all. Here they are.

■ Anticipate difficulties and preteach. Preteaching is covered more fully in Chapter 11, on homework; here I need only say that papers are written better when writing problems are foreseen and solved in advance. They are also read and marked much more quickly than papers full of errors and inadequacies that could have been avoided by preteaching.

■ Make many of your assignments specific and short. By making assignments very specific, so that the class understands exactly what it is supposed to do and why, you will be able to determine quickly, when it comes to marking the papers, whether the assignment has been adequately done. Nothing is more time-consuming than marking a set of papers written on "anything you want."

■ Sometimes read aloud and edit papers in class, before you have spent any time on them. Ask a cross section of students to read their papers aloud, or you read them aloud. Stop after every three or four papers to deal with the most evident errors, weaknesses, strengths, and gems on the board and in discussion. Be careful not to be hard on papers written by timid souls. Encourage students to take some class time to improve their papers in the light of what they are hearing. Then take in the papers, glance at them, just put a check at the top of each to show that you have seen it, and hand them all back with a short spoken comment to the class the next day but with no further reading on your part. If, however, you notice that a student has done a significant piece of creative writing on what was a routine assignment, read and comment on that effort.

■ Base a lesson on common writing problems. Scan an entire set of papers; make no marks, but pick out five or six important common problems and teach a lesson based on these problems the very next day. Before teaching the lesson, hand back the papers so that students may evaluate and revise their own work in relation to the points being discussed.

■ Teach from passages written on the board or duplicated. Read enough papers to find out what the important problems are. Then underline or star certain sentences and passages on certain papers. The next day, explain what you have done and ask the students whose papers you have marked to write the starred or underlined passage on the board *as is,* and use these sentences as the basis for the lesson. It is even better to duplicate these passages, if possible, so that each student may have a copy. Or you can use an overhead projector.

■ Have students form groups, or pairs, to read and react. Small groups allow students to read their papers to others and get reactions—an important aspect of evaluation as well as a rewarding and motivating experience. Talk in advance about what students should be listening for as they hear the papers, and write some items on the board—"Interesting beginning," "Original ideas," "Good description," "Awkward repetitions"—to listen for and to discuss. Students can even evaluate one another's papers, if no one objects.

■ Read a cross section of papers aloud and then have students revise their own papers. On the basis of a quick scan the day before, pick out two good papers, two mediocre ones, and two poor ones, and read them to the class anonymously, discussing and criticizing as you read. Ask students to take notes on the discussion. Then hand all of the papers back, unmarked, and have students examine and revise their own papers in the light of the discussion. This method works especially well when the same topic has been assigned to all students and they can compare their different methods of dealing with the question.

■ "Correct" or edit only part of long papers. If students do long papers, it is sometimes all right to correct carefully and completely only the first two or three pages for spelling and mechanics and to read the remaining pages without making detailed corrections. (From time to time, correct only the last two pages.) Be sure, though, to make comments and suggestions about style, organization, and content that apply to the entire paper.

■ Teach students to proofread their own papers—to try to make themselves strangers to their papers, noting and fixing mistakes and weaknesses as they read and reread, preferably aloud or subvocally "aloud." The distance of a day or two between finishing a paper and proofreading it always helps. Going through this process helps to make students independently good writers. It also saves the teacher hours of time.

Late papers and marks

Handing papers in late is a bad habit. Some teachers mark late papers lower, which is not a good idea if we are really serious about our policy that marks are information, not honors to be bestowed (see Chapter 19). Here is an alternate procedure for late papers.

■ Tell the class that handing papers in when they are due is important for three reasons: students need to learn to be punctual; it is usually better for the class if all papers are evaluated together; and it is more convenient for the teacher. Tell the class that late papers will be marked "late" and so noted in your gradebook.

■ Tell students that even the best of us sometimes cannot meet deadlines. Encourage them, if they are up against more than they can get done, to talk it over with you. Promise to be understanding as long as lateness doesn't get to be a habit. But point out that planning one's time to get work done on time is important, and try to help students learn to do this.

■ When writing a report on a student, if several papers came in late during a marking period note the fact as a piece of information that may properly affect your evaluation of the student's overall performance.

8.

Planning a Year and a Unit

In a moment of enthusiasm, a committee earnestly stated in its minutes, "This year we are going to concentrate on everything." That sentence tells exactly why teaching can be the hardest, the most rewarding, and the most inherently frustrating job there is—because teachers have to try to concentrate on everything and be aware of everything all at once, even though this is impossible.

One part of our concentration must be on the state of mind, body, and spirit of each of our pupils, as well as on their knowledge and experience in the past, present, and near or distant future. Another part is our colleagues in the complex institution where we work. Still another is the community of which our school is a part—both parents and public. And then, of course, we must concentrate on the subject matter we teach. That is the topic of this chapter.

Planning a year's work

Good teachers plan a coherent scheme for a year's work with a class, yet allow for change and evolution as the year proceeds. The year's scheme of content, materials, and activities should be planned, but, as the way opens, we may sometimes depart from our scheme. The subject matter is not the most important element; helping each student to develop into a happy and useful person is. This all-important development takes place best, in schools, as a by-product of dealing with the subject matter. We teach subjects, and the whole business affects students. To say "I teach children, not subjects," expresses a truth, but too often it serves as an excuse for pedagogic wobbliness and loose improvisation, at least in grades four and up.

In most schools, teachers are given a curriculum that is supplied with aims and objectives, divided into units, and furnished with materials. Teachers should become thoroughly familiar with all the elements of the curriculum before the school year begins and make their own plans and arrangements for teaching it. They should try to foresee where their own knowledge can usefully supplement texts and other materials and, where their knowledge is inadequate, to prepare themselves by filling gaps. No teacher should worry about not knowing everything, however. Learning *with* students is good for everyone, provided it is not overdone. Students respect both teachers' knowledge and their willingness to admit gaps in it. Such an admission encourages students to admit that they don't know everything, either, which is motivation for learning more.

A main problem, especially for teachers in the upper grades, is the compulsion to "cover" a certain amount of material. This compulsion, combined with an equal compulsion to be thorough, sometimes leads us into the situation of the student in the cartoon who, frantically writing an exam, glances at the clock and cries, "My God, only five minutes left and three centuries to go!"

We should realize that, while no subject ever gets entirely "covered," students need to feel the satisfaction of having learned a complete section of it. The surveys of American history that never get beyond World War I, or even World War II, are not satisfactory. More important than coverage, in any case, is to develop students' enthusiasm for learning more. If they know how to *do* a subject, rather than just memorizing parts of it, they will be stronger lifelong learners, and that is what being educated is.

A vital part of planning for the year involves thinking carefully about how you are going to help students develop basic skills and attitudes as you work with them and the subject matter. If the school's written curriculum does not list these basics and integrate them into the subjects taught, you would do well to make your own list. One example is the set of basics given in Chapter 5.

Even experienced teachers should take a fresh look each year at what they are teaching to see how adequate and realistic their objectives are and how well they think they are achieving them. Teachers need to devise measures — other than intuition and wishful thinking — suitable to their discipline and style to reveal what their students are achieving. Some suggestions are given in Chapters 16-18 and 21.

Planning a unit of work

As work on skills and attitudes continues throughout the year, students at most grade levels will benefit by the sense of progress they gain by proceeding from unit to unit of subject matter, even if it is only from one chapter or unit in a textbook to the next. Most students like to feel they are starting something new and then completing it, not just keeping on with the same old thing.

It really doesn't matter much whether you have a great theme that arches over all the units in a year's work. Very often, the generalization that such a theme represents exists only in the mind of the teacher. The important thing is to make units interesting and to provide ample materials and activities for learning, backed by a strongly taught strand of skills.

Usually, it makes little difference in what order units are taught, except for the first one, and possibly the last. If you have three or four sections of the same grade, you can teach a different unit to each section during given weeks or months so that your own life will be more varied. That way, you have different papers to read at different times and in smaller batches, and you feel no pressure to keep all four sections going along at exactly the same rate.

Some teachers, however, prefer to unify the work of the entire year under a single theme: the Pilgrims, ecology, ancient Egypt, the family. Teachers in lower and middle grades sometimes use a motif apart from the subject matter to give coherence and interest to the year's work: an African village, with tribes and subtribes, a voyage by ship, a zoo.

In general, a unit should begin with an activity that stimulates students' interest. It should then provide materials and work that maintain that interest and teach the subject matter. A unit should be so constructed that it provides some success to the least able and some challenge to the most gifted. It should be completed with some sort of culminating event — a performance, a discussion, a film accompanied by a writing assignment, or just a challenging final test.

9.

Planning a Class Period

This chapter has to do with planning for a single period, which in most schools lasts between forty and fifty minutes and within which most teachers in the middle and upper grades do their teaching. Schools and classes vary so widely that the following suggestions will not fit all of them.

A typical workable lesson plan

First and most important for each class period is a plan, either sketched in your own brand of shorthand or carefully written out, to get you and the class through from beginning to end. This seventh grade English class plan, while not perfect, illustrates some key points.

1. Write something on the board for the class to start working on. Always put this in the same place so that students will develop the habit of looking for it there.

2. Note reminders to yourself of people and things that need attention whenever convenient during the period.

3. Start the period by letting people who have problems bring them up for discussion. If a problem is of general interest, discuss it with the whole class. If it only concerns the person who raised it, deal with it briefly and offer to see the person at the end of the period—and remember to do so. Keep the question period moving unless problems are general and serious, in which case you may need to abandon part of the lesson plan to get the class on track and motivated.

4. Remind the class of any imminent deadlines—handing in problems, papers, notebooks.

5. Reinforce any rules, formulas, or concepts that people have misunderstood or made errors on in the past day or two.

6. Now the really new stuff of the lesson begins. Often it is better to start at this point, omitting the earlier items or working them in later. It all depends on the mood of the class, what the students expect, how interested they are in the material, and what you have been doing the two or three days before. Some classes like a change of pace; others do better with an unvarying, reassuring pattern.

7. Note the questions you want to ask the class. Asking varied general and specific questions is one of the most important parts of teaching.

8. For a change of pace, give a short written exercise to be done in class, and save time to read some examples aloud.

9. In case the period hasn't ended (usually it has by this time), have enough games or activities ready to take as little or as much time as you need.

The six most important aspects of this lesson plan are that it is definite and purposeful; it allows students to bring up problems that may be causing difficulty in their long-term work; it contains more material than you can possibly cover and yet does not seem cut off if not completed; it covers new specific material while referring to previous ideas and skills and looking forward to new ones; it gives every member of the class, whether nimble or slow, an opportunity to participate; and it offers enough change of pace so that the class is unlikely to get bored.

Arranging and teaching a class period

Developing study skills and arranging for homework, or independent work, are obviously vital ingredients of the class period and of the year's work in school. Before discussing them in the next two chapters, however, here are a few more ideas for planning your work.

■ Establish routines. The sooner you set up basic routines for getting materials, handing papers back to students, students handing in work, arranging conferences, breaking into small groups, and having a place where homework assignments are written, the more freedom you and the class will have for teaching and learning. Always be open to students' ideas for better ways to carry out routines.

■ Every period may be a fresh start for someone in the class. To maintain a truly professional and humane attitude toward each pupil, each teacher must teach with all the school's past experience with that pupil in mind, yet allow constantly for the possibility that a student may, under our influence, or the influence of the summer, or something just said or read, be reawakened or inspired—any day, any minute. If you are going to err in your plans for a students, err on the side of optimism and high expectations.

■ Don't worry about unfinished discussion. Learning and thought do not stop when the bell rings. If what has happened during class has stimulated interest, that may have been its main value, even if you never get back to the question again. If the bell does ring when the class is in the middle of talking about something important, make a note to give it first priority the next day.

■ Save lesson plans that work well. Some teachers, at the end of the year, throw away all their old lesson plans, tests, and devices with the admirable purpose of avoiding clutter, staleness, doing it better next year, being open to new ways. If a book, test, plan, game, or exercise works well, keep it and use it again. For several years I taught the same three books to the eighth grade. They all worked well; I developed and refined multiple-choice tests on each, found which discussion questions were provocative, and invented written assignments that stimulated good writing. I became so familiar with the material that I was liberated—liberated to observe my students, attend to their needs, see them after school. Once knowing the subject matter, I was freed to know my students.

■ Don't be afraid now and then to toss out your plan and ask, "All right, what would you like to talk about today?" If you let students know that you will be doing this occasionally, some of them may come to you and say, "Can't we talk about . . . sometime?" and you can make whatever it is part of your plan within the next few days. Some teachers find it useful to keep a "Things we need to talk about" box somewhere in the room that only the teacher can open.

■ Have a large clock in the room so that everyone can know what time it is and plan accordingly.

■ Reserve the first or last ten minutes (or more) of certain periods as reading and consultation time, when all students know that they are to have some independent, silent work to do, and that they have a chance, if they need it, to talk with you. This is an excellent way to get individual papers dealt with and small problems straightened out. An alternative is to set aside one entire period each week for reading and consultation.

■ Have a sign-up place on the chalkboard for people who want or need to talk with you about a problem or individual business, like a puzzling math problem. Or you can write people's names there if you need to see them. This way, nobody has to wait in line; when one name is crossed off, the next person comes forward. When you are dealing with the sign-up list, be sure the rest of the class knows that they are expected to work quietly in their seats.

■ Everyone should always have independent work to do—reading, writing, figuring—if a few free minutes crop up. For those who have forgotten to come prepared, have a collection of books and activities available.

■ Develop some foolproof time passers in case plans fail, half the class gets held in gym, or textbooks haven't come, or just if life looks too grim for regular work.

■ Plan to finish class business early from time to time so that you can declare a relaxed moment for the class to talk freely or start on homework, with you circulating about the room.

■ Schedule, either regularly or when the time and climate are right, brief-feature time (show and tell), when individual students may take a minute or two to tell, explain, act, mime, or show something of special interest, tell a joke, or ask a question. Having a sign-up sheet will let you know whether there is enough to fill the time. Items need not have anything to do with classwork, though they may add to its scope. You, too, should sign up occasionally.

■ Have one day every week or two be presentation day, when some new material—film, video, skit, lecture, reading aloud, speaker, debate, oral report, a new idea, lesson, or subject matter—is presented and the class mainly listens, takes notes, and asks questions.

■ Reserve a day, perhaps once every two weeks, when students spend all or part of the period writing or doing problems or other exercises and then hand their work in at the end of the period. This gives you a check on how well students work under pressure of time and without outside help. They may either all work on the same thing or not, as you judge best.

■ Identify as many students' problems as early as possible so that you and your colleagues can get to work on them. Too many teachers say, "Oh, I never look at a student's record. I want to give each one a fresh start and not be biased." Unfortunately, this often means that they don't find out until too late who is a poor reader and who reads well; who always slumps between Christmas and midyear unless held firm; who is dumb and acts bright; who is bright and acts dumb; who works best when left alone; who would come to life if you would just come out to cheer at the game after school; who needs to talk but is too shy to say so. Ignoring such matters means that essential information is rediscovered only by January, fully understood in February, and brought to the point of action in March, by which time it is so close to June that we decide just to write a note about it for next year's teachers. We have no right to repeat such mistakes. It is unprofessional, inefficient, and not even respectful. It is much better to discover from the files or from colleagues problems that need remedial action in October to leave time to diagnose the trouble, prescribe treatment, and get to work.

■ After the school year is under way, or perhaps during the last two or three months of the year, let students develop a plan for independent work or independent projects. (Chapter 11 gives specific suggestions for setting guidelines and monitoring progress of projects.) The class may agree that one or two periods a week will be project days, or that an entire week can be turned over to project work, or that no homework can be given for a certain time because they are doing project work at home. Some students will want and be ready for more independent work than others, and some will be doing it on their own without special scheduling help.

10.

Study Skills

When students are assigned independent work, or homework, they should be left on their own to do the work in their own way and according to their own plans. They often need help, however. Many students need to be taught some study skills, which is another term for "how to learn." Others, who seem to know how to study from the very start, are understandably bored to death by study-habit formulas.

A statement for students

Here is a statement on study skills that works for students in grades 4-12. (Permission to duplicate it for student use is hereby granted.) It can be taught piecemeal, which might be best for fourth, fifth, and sixth graders, or it can be handed out to each student and then discussed with those who show signs that they might benefit from it. You may well require students to read, discuss, and understand the statement, but no one should be required to abide by it, point by point. Students' minds work in ways far too varied to justify forced conformity to a system of study skills.

Study Skills

How to "study" is not a simple lesson, easily learned. Also, we all have our own style of learning. Some of us work in bursts, some plod along systematically. Some reason along straight lines of logic, some leap intuitively from insight to insight.

If you are not doing well in school, or are doing well but could be doing even better, this list of study techniques may help you. You probably won't want to use them all, but some will almost certainly be useful to you.

1. *Write down assignments, with date due, in a regular place,* like a homework notebook, not on a scrap of paper. If you aren't sure what the assignment means, ask the teacher.

2. *Have a regular schedule for home study.* When you get home from school, your mind may need a rest and your body some food and exercise. Styles and rhythms of brainwork and body work differ; use the schedule that works best for you.

3. *Have a regular place to study* equipped with pencils, pen, paper, scissors, ruler, dictionary, calendar, and a lamp. Occasionally an escape from the regular place can provide new inspiration—under a tree, on the roof.

4. *Be certain of the purpose of an assignment before you do it.* Ask yourself "What am I supposed to learn from this? Why was it assigned?" Teachers almost always have a particular goal in mind when they give an assignment. What is it? If you don't know, ask.

5. *Skim over a reading assignment before reading it closely.* Don't just read the assignment from start to finish. First, glance at the main headings and titles, or paragraph beginnings, to get a general idea of what it is about and to help you relate the ideas to the main topic, to the rest of the course, and to whatever other knowledge you have, when you read the chapter closely later. This skimming shouldn't take more than four or five minutes for a fifteen- to twenty-page chapter.

6. *Use whatever study aids the textbook offers* if you have some close reading to do. Note the chapter title, which will probably give you the main idea, and the subheads within the chapter. If words are italicized, read them with special care. Look closely at lists or paragraphs signaled by numbers, "bullets," or other signposts. Be sure you know—or try to figure out—why the author has included whatever charts, maps, and pictures are in the book. Go over questions and exercises at the ends of chapters; these usually stress and recapitulate the main ideas.

7. *Pause after each paragraph or section to see if you can recall its main ideas.* If you cannot, reread the passage. This pausing to recall and review is one of the best ways to fix ideas in your mind. (You don't do this with novels or stories, because you don't read them for mastery of information.)

8. *Mark your book if you own it.* Don't just sit back and let the words come at you. Use a pencil as you read to mark things you want to remember.

9. *Look up new words.* Keep a dictionary handy. After you have looked up

a word, try to use it a couple of times in the next day or two to implant it in your mind and to see if it works. Try not to look up so many words at any one time that it breaks into your train of thought.

10. *When you have finished an assignment, try to recall the main ideas, perhaps writing them down.* This is a quick way to fix ideas in your mind and to show where you need to reread. Don't just heave a sigh of relief and close the book when you reach the last word. Try to answer end-of-chapter questions. If you cannot, review the section involved.

11. *Remember, there are different kinds of reading for different kinds of assignments.* Get your mind set for the kind of reading you think applies.

a. Skimming—for an overview of the material or to find specific items of information.

b. Rapid, relaxed reading—for a story or an account of something that interests you.

c. Close, active reading—for mastery in using textbooks, encyclopedias, and other materials containing detailed information and ideas.

d. Word-for-word reading, perhaps aloud—for directions or for math and science problems.

e. Poetry reading (best done aloud)—for meaning, metaphor, feeling, and sound.

12. *Note and study all corrections and suggestions* made in class and on your papers. If the teacher makes a correction on your paper or a suggestion to you in class, that's important, because it is something directed at you that the teacher thinks you particularly need. Don't let it pass. Note also any suggestions made to the class as a whole. If the teacher thinks something is worth mentioning specially, it's probably important, and teachers have a way of emphasizing in class what they are likely to give tests on later. You don't have to agree with teachers' suggestions, corrections, or opinions of what is important, but it is wise to try to understand their thinking as well as you can.

13. *Plan your time if you have a long-term assignment.* For instance, if you have three weeks to do a report on a large subject, divide your time, perhaps spending the first week doing rough organization and collecting materials, the next week reading the materials and taking notes, and the third week reorganizing and then writing your report and proofreading it. Don't put off the work until the last few days. You may find yourself without material and without time to search for it.

14. *When doing an assignment, note any points on which you aren't clear* and raise them in class at the beginning of the next period. This is a good way to learn.

15. *Learn to make a rough outline.* An outline is a valuable tool for organizing your ideas for a writing assignment or for reviewing materials you have studied. If your teachers have not taught you how to outline, you can find a section on this in almost any English textbook. It's a waste of time, however, to spend hours making a perfectly formed outline for an ordinary assignment or review. The important thing is to get the main ideas and the sub-ideas stated briefly and arranged logically.

16. *When you review for tests, don't reread everything.* Instead, use the study aids in your books, the marks you have made, and any notes you have taken on your reading or on what the teacher has emphasized. *Spend your time on the parts you don't know.*

17. *Your basic obligation to your work is to be interested in it.* Try not to set up a block between you and your education by saying, "I'm bored," or "It's stupid." You have a perfect right to feel this way, but if you let the feeling control your actions, you may fail to learn. Instead, make yourself find something in the work that can catch your interest.

Using these seventeen points in studying will take a little more time when you first go over your material, but the total amount of time taken will be less, and your mastery of the work will be more efficient. However, if you have a system of your own that you think works better than this one, and you are doing well in school, ignore these suggestions and go on using your own system.

Study habits we call "odd"

We run the danger of imposing on students our own ideas of the right and proper way to learn and to schoolwork, only to find that it simply goes against the nature of some. Many people do not learn systematically, step by step, with a plan, at a steady pace. Let's look at several kinds of students who may do well in school, but in their own "peculiar" ways. None of these habits is exclusive to any individual; the same person may exhibit several of them, depending on the material involved or on other things going on in their lives at the time.

Slow shifters are students who require considerable time to warm up to a task and get involved in it but who, when involved, progress powerfully through the task and hate to stop until it is done. They don't want to break for supper, they may want to stay up way past their bedtime — until finished. They don't like to jump from bit to bit and are slow to shift away from whatever task is absorbing them.

Moody workers sometimes feel like doing homework and sometimes don't. Their currents of mood run deep and cause what seem like sea changes. When the waters are right for joking or dreaming or sleeping, they joke, dream, talk, or sleep, and when they are right for working, they outwork anyone else. These students often do poorly in scheduled study halls.

Physical learners are those for whom a desk and chair are a prison, those who read best while pacing, who write in a burst, then take a turn around the room or downstairs or around the house, and then come back to burst again.

Talkers are the students who, if they have to read something to master it, want to talk about it, argue about it, say what they think, find out what others think. They bother their parents or brothers and sisters with talk or spend much of their homework time on the telephone. Their minds are turned on and their thinking stimulated by verbal exchange. By this means they learn well. Without it, they languish.

Slow learners are not stupid but need plenty of time to assimilate material and accomplish their work. They may do well, even brilliantly, but they can't do it fast. Often they are thorough, sometimes they argue with and think about a book, or a test item, as they go. They just can't be rushed. If they are, they don't finish, or they finish poorly. (A survey of Phi Beta Kappa members showed that students who excel academically do not tend to be exceptionally fast readers.) Teachers and parents err seriously when they equate slowness with dullness or stupidity and when they equate speed with intelligence. Very often the brightest students take the longest time to do a piece of homework that involves creativity because they are aware, as less able students are not, of the many possibilities it offers for accomplishment and pleasure.

Last-minute artists are the students, so annoying to plodders, who get a long-term assignment and then apparently go carefree until the last moment, when, after an all-night orgy of reading and writing, produce in what seems like a couple of hours the paper that took most people three weeks. It is hard not to look at such papers with a resentful eye. We must force ourselves to read and evaluate each paper for what it is, not for how it was prepared.

Bucklers under pressure get nervous if they are hurried. They like to have work assigned well in advance and to proceed systematically until it is done — often well before it is due, never late. They buckle mentally and do poorly if hurried.

Cramped-hand kids find the act of writing slow torture. They should learn to use a typewriter or word processor. They may also do better if allowed to give up cursive writing and go back to "printing" separate letters. After a few days of practice, the change to printing speeds up the handwriting of this kind of student.

Therefore, while we should instruct our students in techniques of study and mastery, we must be careful never to force them into a style of learning that is contrary to their natures. If we do, some could fail, do less well, and even develop a much poorer opinion of themselves than necessary.

A better approach is to say, "Here are some study skills that work well for many people. If they work for you, fine. If they don't, then make your own system. If you have trouble doing that, we can talk about it." It is also reassuring to describe some of the successful "different" — a better word than "odd" — styles given above. Students who recognize themselves in one or more of these can say, "That's me!" and feel much better.

Young students, and their parents, tend to have such reverence for standard study habits solemnly pronounced by the teacher that they go to damaging lengths to conform or to require their children to conform. If students are having trouble doing independent work, try to find time to talk with them and their parents. Find out exactly how they go about the job, what is causing them trouble, and help them figure out ways that will work for them.

11.
Homework

Most people believe in homework and seem to think that it has an almost magic power. In fact, some people even judge the quality of a school by the amount of homework it gives. This is much too simple a basis for judgment, and a lot of exercises done at home merely as busywork can be one of the worst parts of school in a child's life. I remember a student who, when told by her parents to turn off the radio while doing her homework, said, "But I have to have something to keep my mind on while I'm doing this stupid stuff." (Also, radio music for some people provides a kind of "white sound" that covers up the distracting noises of family life at home.)

Why homework?

In a well-taught class, the subject and skills being learned should be important, appealing, and demanding enough to carry over into the time outside of school. At its best, homework grows out of continuing interest and work. It should not be a dose prescribed against idleness but a vital extension of learning begun at school.

"Homework" really is a misnomer. "Independent work" or "directed independent study" are better terms. This kind of work, much of which may be done at home, can serve one or more of the following purposes: to give the student a chance to practice and master skills or content taught at school; to encourage or require independent creativity in writing, projects, research, crafts, or art; to encourage or require wide independent reading; to provide time for reading "study" material in subjects like history; to provide opportunity for independent science or art projects; and to further classroom discussion.

Never, though, let your teaching plan fall into a pattern of having students do most of their learning at home and using class time for recitation, which is usually boring, or testing. Too often teachers simply say, "All right, for tomorrow learn the material on pages 37-52 and write a one-page essay on it." In such a situation, who is doing the teaching? The parents, or the poor students, struggling alone or together on the telephone, teaching themselves. Too often little real teaching gets done at all, and very little learning occurs, except learning to feel frustrated.

Preteaching

When you assign specific homework, it helps greatly if you anticipate problems and difficulties students are likely to have with it and then preteach—teach students what they need to know to do the assignment well, rather than having it be an exercise in making mistakes and reinforcing bad habits.

Too many of us say, in effect, "Here's the assignment; now go do it." Then, when the time comes to read and mark homework, we are surprised and discouraged by the poor quality of the work, by how many students made mistakes they shouldn't have made, by how many failed to see or take advantage of seemingly obvious possibilities for creativity, or even by the sad fact that some could not do the assignment at all—or chose not to.

You think you're discouraged; the students are probably even more discouraged. After all, it is they, not you, who failed to perform well and whose work is being evaluated.

Students can always learn from their mistakes, and a post mortem can show them how to do better next time. Even so, it is much easier for everyone if you can predict what problems and simple mistakes are likely to be and to teach how to deal with them when they crop up. That way, students get practice in doing things right, and they feel better about their work when they hand it in and when you hand it back. And it saves you having to correct the same mistakes on paper after paper.

So, before turning students loose on an assignment, especially a major one, try to show them what they need to do to succeed. You can do this in two phases. A typical writing sample, applicable to any subject, will serve as an example.

1. *Let students ask.* Ask students what problems they think they may encounter in doing the assignment and then discuss as necessary. Here are questions they might ask.

"What do I write about?" Suggest a specific topic or two, ask others in the class to add topics, and offer to talk later with anyone who is really stuck.

"Where do I get the information I'll need?" Again, discuss and suggest. One source students often ignore is their own ideas and experience or those of people they know.

"How long does it have to be?" Avoid setting an exact length, unless writing to a specified length is part of the assignment. Whatever the suggested length, always stress that what one says is more important than how long it takes to say it.

"How do I get started? I always have trouble starting." Suggest that quite often people do best by just beginning to write freely—even if what they first write later turns out to be the middle of the paper—without editing or worrying. Then they can go over what they have written and rearrange it, if need be. Or they can write about an important point or two and add a few sentences on their significance. Often best, they can make a rough outline of their ideas and then begin to write. Remind students that most serious writers throw away or radically revise a lot of what they have written once they get going.

"How will the assignment be graded?" Will you be giving one mark or several? Will you comment on the homework? Explain exactly what your plan is and ask whether it seems fair. Tell how you are going to evaluate content (quality, quantity, relevance, organization), spelling, punctuation, and so forth.

"Will our papers be read aloud to the class?" Ask the class how it feels, but don't necessarily be limited by the answers you get. Some people benefit by having their work shared, even though they don't request it. Talk about the audience for the paper—is it the teacher? the class? a small group or one other person in the class? others?

2. *Teach the students.* Even after all questions have been discussed some things may still need to be taught before the work is assigned completely. You should have thought through the assignment in advance and perhaps even done it yourself, noting any problems that might crop up. Here are a few typical ones.

Spelling. If you see any familiar troublemakers on the horizon, write them on the board and quickly point out the problems. If the students are writing about an "embarrassing" experience, for example, teach the two a's, double r, and double s.

Mechanics. If the assignment involves written dialogue or other specially presented material, remind the class of the rules involved—paragraphing, punctuation, indenting, symbols. You can even have the students copy a sample from the board, if you think that might help, or refer them to the relevant part of their textbook.

Organization. Many writing assignments involve essays, which require arranging ideas in coherent order and subordinating topics and subtopics convincingly. This skill needs to be taught again and again because some students are slow to learn it, and others are quick to forget or ignore it. A straight-out lesson or two can be useful, either for the entire class or for those who especially need it.

First and second drafts and revisions. You may need to remind some students of the value of writing a first draft, then making revisions—a single word here, a sentence there, order, emphasis, beginning and ending, or whatever else doesn't sound right and interesting. You might hand out a sample for the class to revise together as you all think aloud about it. Urge students to be highly critical strangers to their own work—to get outside it, and be hard on it.

Proofreading. Make it clear whether you accept crossed-out and corrected words or require a completely neat copy. It can be a discouraging waste of time for students to have to copy a page over just because of a few errors that can be easily and legibly fixed.

Schedule. When making any assignment, but especially a long one, discuss the timetable for completing it. As a useful form of preteaching, you may suggest, or require, that work be shown to you at various stages—notes, preliminary draft, first draft, and so on. If students run into problems at any stage, you may need to sit down and talk about them.

One last word about preteaching: sometimes it is hard to judge whether you have done too much of it. If you foresee and deal with every possible problem, you may be taking the joy of discovery out of the assignment. Remember, some mistakes are worth making for the lessons they teach. Sometimes it is best to let students, especially able and highly motivated ones, rush forth and err and learn thus not to err again.

Another danger, especially with timid and academically weak students, is to load an assignment with so many cautions and warnings that they become paralyzed. Yet another possibility is preteaching to the point of boredom. Preteach only bits, and only the essential bits. It is better to let enthusiastic students fling themselves into an assignment while they are still excited and deal with problems later than to try to ensure dead conformity and competence in advance.

Making the purpose of homework clear

When students ask, "Why do we have to do this? I don't see the point," we too often answer, "Because it will help you," or "Because you should do your homework," or "Because I say so." So the students, if they are dutiful, go through the motions with no understanding of what they are doing and how it fits into a larger objective worth accomplishing.

Instead, we should try to show why the work is important and worth doing, even if the reward is somewhat removed in time. Sometimes this is done best by discussion. "Why is this assignment important to do? What are you likely to learn from it?" We need to keep cultivating an understanding of the larger context in which specific pieces of work are done. A sense of context can have enormous influence on learning and morale.

It is not enough to have a grand scheme in our own minds; it must be in the minds of our students, as well. When someone asks, "Why do we have to do this?" turn the question to the class. Sometimes it is useful even to say, "If you aren't convinced that this is worth doing, then you don't have to do it—but you've got to let me try to convince you before I allow you to say no."

Some more suggestions about homework

While some of the following suggestions may seem fairly obvious, they can make life easier for you and your students in the long run.

■ Do not require perfect neatness on practice exercises. Many school tasks are not worth doing neatly.

■ Always write homework assignments down, and always put them in the same place—either in the same place on the board, for short ones, or the same place in the room, for more complicated assignments that have been duplicated and distributed.

■ Keep in touch with other teachers so that too many of you do not load on lots of work or tests all at once. Listen to your students; they will let you know when this happens.

■ Never use homework as a punishment.

■ Try to assign homework a week or more at a time, with due dates noted, so that students may learn to plan their time and take advantage of slack time in one subject to work on another.

■ Accept plausible excuses for homework not done—but not too many. Students often have legitimate reasons for not getting their work done, and you should recognize these.

■ Don't require, or encourage your school to require, a definite amount of homework each day—sixth grade, an hour and a half; seventh and eighth grade, two hours; ninth and tenth grade, three hours. The point of homework is to do it and benefit from it. Some students will do it well and fast, some slowly and poorly. The job well done, not the time spent doing it, is the main thing.

■ Allow for a range of responses in as many assignments as you can to challenge able students yet allow the less able to find some degree of success in their work.

■ Be sure not to give assignments that invite plagiarism. For example, an assignment to write a report on George Washington's boyhood is a poor one, since probably an excellent account of that subject is already written and available in the *World Book, The Book of Knowledge,* or *The Encyclopaedia Britannica.* An intelligent student may well look up the encyclopedia article, mess it up and rearrange it enough so that it won't count as "violation of copyright" or plagiarism, and then find two or three biographies of Washington so that there can be a bibliography and a few footnotes. But basically there is no research or original thinking involved. Better, assign a topic on which no one has written, such as "George Washington's Boyhood and My Father's Boyhood Compared." Don't assign "Lizards" as a topic, or "Frogs." But "Lizards and Frogs, Similarities and Differences" might be good; or "Observations and Comparisons of Two Fish and Two Animals at Our House." Major homework assignments should require some original thought.

Contracts

In some schools, long-term independent work is done according to a contract, which can be used by students in grade 5 and up. A contract is simply a signed agreement between student and teacher under which the student is to accomplish a certain task or amount of work in a given subject by a certain time.

Contracts are a good way to get students involved in making decisions about their own work and how they are going to do it. They are also help in tailoring work to individual students' interests and capacities. If your classroom is well furnished with materials and has a cooperative atmosphere, contracts can put students on their own while you spend time giving individual instruction.

The terms of a simple contract—which begins by naming the student, the teacher, the work to be accomplished, and the date by which the work is to be completed—may consist of (1) reading to be done, (2) other investigation to be done, (3) writing to be done, (4) hoped-for benefits from completing the work, and (5) how contracted work will be evaluated or graded.

Sometimes a contract may seem reasonable at first but later turn out to be too hard or not challenging enough. Since contracts work only if students can complete them with reasonable diligence, their terms should always be open to change. Mistakes in judgment, if discussed and rectified, can be real learning opportunities. Periodic progress checks between student and teacher are desirable so that problems may be spotted and dealt with before they get out of hand.

It usually works best if only part of class time is spent on contract work. Students like to know when they will be doing contract work and when they will be doing work of other kinds. Contract work often spills over into homework; some students may wish to do contract work entirely on their own.

74

Independent projects

An independent project differs from a contract only in degree. With older students in a flexible school, such a project may even involve being allowed to leave school one day a week or for certain periods on certain days.

Independent projects that fail usually do so because it has not been made clear how they are to be carried out or evaluated, and because they are not carefully and regularly monitored. For monitoring, a definite, written timetable for checking progress and phases of accomplishment works best. We can take a six-week period as an example.

Using a simple form, entitled "Progress Report" and giving start and end dates, students rate themselves each Friday, for six Fridays, according to one of the following statements: (1) "I am doing well, am on schedule, have no problems"; (2) "I am making progress but need to discuss"; (3) "I have real problems and may have to shift projects"; (4) "I have nearly finished my project"; or (5) "Other (describe)." Students may add explanations, as they wish. The following Monday, the teacher returns the forms to students, with written comments, and sets up conferences as needed. In this way, students are not left on their own, possibly to flounder or fail.

Homework and parents

Parents often ask teachers how involved they should get in their children's homework. In general, we can ask parents to do the following things.

■ If you can, provide proper conditions for study — space, equipment, and time.

■ Homework is independent work, so be sure your children do it independently. If they are unable to do it, tell them to ask their teacher.

■ Never do homework for your children. This teaches them very little and is only likely to hide from teachers what they need to know about weakness or lack of understanding to be able to teach what is needed. In other words, never shield your children from the legitimate consequences of not doing their job. If, on the other hand, there are no consequences when you feel there should be some, ask your child's teacher for a conference.

■ Be a source of information, if you can; better, tell your children where they can find information on their own.

■ If you can straighten out a simple matter of fact or misunderstanding with a little teaching of your own, go ahead, but be careful not to teach too much or teach a trick that shortcuts understanding, as with with mathematics, where answer-getting tricks work up to a point but not beyond.

■ Don't force your children to do homework. Many students get their homework done in free periods or study halls at school.

■ Because children learn in many different ways, don't expect your children to learn in the same ways that you do.

■ It is all right for students to talk about their homework on the telephone. In fact, it is one of the best ways to learn, as long as they are really exchanging ideas, not answers, aren't imposing on the good will and intelligence of their friends, and aren't hogging the phone.

12.

Organizing and Managing the People

It is easy to write this chapter about organizing and managing the people with whom a teacher has to deal, and then to offer, in the next three chapters, ideas about organizing the place, the materials, and time. It is far less easy to separate these things in your classroom, because everything affects everything else.

Class size

It seems, after experiments with the size and shape of classrooms and the number of students in them, that it is almost in the very nature of people and spaces that students and teachers should be brought together in a ratio of about 25:1, enclosed by four classroom walls. Why?

A group of twenty-five is about the largest in which people can view themselves as a group, talk among themselves without whispering or shouting, and move and pass things around quickly. A group much larger than twenty-five is too public to work well, and a group much smaller makes inefficient use of a skilled teacher's time and salary in most schools.

Many people are convinced that class size correlates directly with successful learning. However, most studies fail to show that each student in a well-taught class of ten to fifteen students will learn more than in a well-taught class of twenty to twenty-five, or even thirty. Also, it is clear that a poor teacher with thirty students will be a poor teacher with fifteen students. There is a limit to acceptable size; I would put it at about thirty, and I would put the optimum size at about twenty.

Another factor is each teacher's "pupil load." In middle schools and high schools, a pupil load of eighty students per teacher in a public school might be considered ideal, but 100 students is not too large; in independent schools, this figure is closer to sixty-five. To make it work, though, you need efficient record keeping and access to files, a strong sense of high expectations of all students by the staff, a school climate conducive to learning, and a school rule that students must meet academic requirements to be promoted.

Since at least 90 per cent of all students and teachers are grouped for schoolwork in classrooms, the suggestions here are based on the prevailing pattern of school organization. They are open to whatever alterations ingenious readers might wish to make.

Some elements of organization

Organization and management, and enthusiasm for and ability to learn — or the lack of these — originate within each person. Our purpose as teachers should be to help each student become a more organized, self-managing, enthusiastically learning person, even if only gradually, and never uniformly. Some students will never achieve this goal, while others will have achieved it before we ever meet them. Our job is to do our best to arrange things so that we and our students can live and learn together.

The simplest and most usual way to organize and manage a class is as a single group, with everyone expected to do the same work at the same time. It is possible to combine a great deal of individual work with an all-class approach if you are skillful in the way you make and deal with assignments.

You can modify the whole-class approach by breaking the group up into smaller groups or by having all students work on their own. The best cues to any method of grouping come from the needs of your students, the requirements of your school, and your own abilities, training, personality, and temperament. Here are some ideas to keep in mind, no matter what methods you use.

1. *Monitoring.* You, as the teacher, are responsible for keeping track of the academic, social, psychological, and physical situation of each stu-

dent. You should know fairly well whether each student is "on task." You hear what students say or don't say. You read and deal with what students write and keep a record of it. You see what they are reading. You find ways for them to record and share with you and one another their progress and problems. You know where they are, or are supposed to be, at all times. You do your best to see who is bored and who is overchallenged. And you give tests, formal and informal, to keep track of who is falling behind and who needs special help. A careful system of monitoring is especially important in a classroom where students work on their own much of the time, because it is so easy for students to go out to pasture. Chapters 16, 18, and 21 suggest various types of monitoring.

2. *Groups.* Students like to work in groups as a change from always meeting as a class. Elementary school teachers have long been expert at making and managing groups, especially to teach reading. Most subjects lend themselves to differentiated homework and reading and writing assignments, making it possible to avoid straight ability grouping and the bad effects it can have. In subjects involving sequential skills, such as foreign language and mathematics, ability grouping is probably necessary unless the work is mostly individual. The bad effects of ability grouping can be reduced by allowing for elective units, some of which are homogeneously grouped. Here are some ways to set up groups with frequently changing membership.

Random groups. For groups of five, or four, count "1-2-3-4-5" or "1-2-3-4" around the room and tell each group where to meet.

Interest groups. If your room is arranged in interest centers (see Chapter 13), let students sign up for their interests and needs, listing three in order of preference, and then set up groups of similar size. Later, when new groups are formed, those who did not get their first-choice interest before may now be given preference.

Named groups. Younger students enjoy belonging to a group with a name—one they choose themselves—or groups that temporarily call themselves villages, tribes, or teams.

Editing or correcting groups. These can be groups of three, or even just pairs, to deal with one another's written work or other work before it gets handed in or shown to the class. You can count these groups off in such a way that best friends and habitual sitters-together can be separated.

Discussion panel. In preparing for an assignment, it can sometimes help to have a panel of students discuss the subject and stir up ideas and questions and write them down. After the panel has talked for about five minutes and written down their questions about the assignment, you can open the discussion to the whole class, with you presiding.

Dispersal groups. If you have a stable class population, it saves time to form groups in advance, seeing to it that each group has some able people in it and someone who can act as chairman. Make a list of these groups and post it so that when you say "Disperse," the class can go quickly into small-group work. This plan works well for discussion, brainstorming, sharing, writing, and other work that needs a small audience.

"Sides." A classic but very poor method for organizing a class into teams is to have two captains "choose up sides." This makes some students feel rejected as the pool of the unchosen dwindles. Far better to use the random "1-2-1-2" system of counting off.

3. *Panel of "experts."* Most classes have students who are especially good at certain parts of the work. Since time is always short for helping students individually, you can have "experts" in spelling, fractions, research techniques, handling clay, chosen by you, by the class, or by themselves as volunteers. Post their names so that people will know whom to see when the time comes. You will need to keep an eye on things to be sure that the "experts" have expertise and that they aren't just showing off, being dictators, or simply fooling around with a friend.

4. *Always something to do.* In any classroom not entirely dominated by up-front teaching, there are inevitably times when students run out of things to do and find themselves at loose ends. While sitting around doing nothing, talking, and looking out the window aren't terrible, it is still a good idea to have something ready for anyone who runs out of work, like reading, research, or other activity available, preferably changed each day, or a series of "job boxes," from which students may pick out a piece of work and do it.

5. *Silence bell.* Sometimes, when the class is working in groups, you need a quick way to lower the noise level or get complete quiet. Shouting over the class may just make things worse and everyone nervous. Much more neutral is a bell, one that makes a single sharp "ding"—one ding for "Lower the noise level," and two for "Quiet, please. I have something to say." Use the bell sparingly.

6. *Students teaching students.* Students can teach classmates or students in other grades. Younger students tend to learn a great deal when slightly older students teach them individually, for they receive the "teacher's" total attention and feel much freer to ask one other person questions than they do in front of an entire class. Perhaps it is the student teachers who learn the most. When they know they are going to have to teach something, they know they have to learn it themselves, and they learn it well.

7. *Beware of organization by labels.* We tend to "organize" students in our minds by label—"He's *bright*"—that group; "She's *limited*"—that group; "He's *learning-disabled*"—that group; "She's *from a single-parent family*"—that group; "His *parents interfere*"—that group; "She's a *faculty child*"—that group. While it may be useful for us to know all these things about our students, we should know them about each student as an individual, not primarily or automatically as a way of grouping students for special group treatment.

13.

Organizing the Place

This chapter assumes that most classrooms are large enough to permit some variety of arrangement and that the chairs and desks are not bolted to the floor in rows. But even if your room is filled with bolted rows, and each row with students, with the overflow sitting on the window sills, do read this chapter quickly for an idea or two about using walls and odd spaces. Because organizing the place is closely related to organizing the materials, this chapter and the next may be read almost as one.

Ideas that work

Set up your room as attractively and workably as you can well before your first class meets in the fall. Once physical order is established, the class can talk and write about it and decide what to do with it: "What is the best way to arrange students, teacher, and furniture?" "How can we fix our room up better?"

You can draw various seating arrangements on the board — circle, square, clusters, groups of four desks, row — and ask the students to talk about the advantages and disadvantages of each scheme, in various situations. Even if you don't want the class to discuss these questions, put them to yourself and ask other teachers what they think. Constructive as it may be to ask students and other teachers about arranging and equipping the classroom, you are the one who has to live in it and with it. Respect your own needs; you are the one who is there all day, day in and day out.

Which of the following suggestions you can and want to use depends on the size of your room, class, and budget, the kind of school you are in, and the kind of person you are. Some things that seem suitable only for elementary school may surprise you when you try them out on older students, who spend far too much time in dull, sloppy, sterile classrooms.

1. *Special spots.* Having special spots in the room can save time and avoid useless talk and wandering. Here are some.

Homework. You can have a special place on the board where homework assignments are always written.

"Look here first." Some teachers like to have classes always look in a certain place the minute they come into the room for a statement they can try to prove or disprove, a quotation they can discuss, an exercise to do before class starts, a joke, or a surprise.

Word list. If the class is working on something that involves special vocabulary, or if interesting words come up, you can have a special place for writing these words, with short definitions, so that everyone may see them, and leave them up for a few days.

Hand-in box. Having a box makes it possible for students to turn in papers and other written work without having to hunt for you.

Message and hand-back box. It sometimes helps to make a file folder or large envelope for each student, with the name clearly marked. When you have a paper to return, a message to give, or special individual assignments to make, you put the item in the student's envelope and leave it in the hand-back box. After emptying their envelopes, students leave them in the box for future use.

Bulletin boards. Most classrooms have bulletin boards, but usually not enough, and almost always dull. Besides being a stimulus for activities and projects, bulletin boards can reward interesting work by displaying it. You can have a contest to see who comes up with the best ideas for enlivening bulletin boards or a "special feature" space in which to post students' work for a day or two. The special feature place must be really special, or students won't look at it. By the way, it's an excellent way to encourage students who need a boost. Many classrooms ignore the three feet of wall just below the ceiling as another area for bulletin boards.

For room-to-room teachers. In many schools, short space and complex schedules make it impossible for some teachers to have their own classrooms. They teach a period here and a period there. For teachers who work under these conditions, here are two suggestions.

Stake out a claim to a small part of the room, the wall, and the chalkboard space that everyone knows is yours. Here you can write assignments and "look here first" items and display at least a bit of student work.

Carry a bit of your "place" with you—student folders, hand-in box, and whatever other items you and your students use to keep routines going easily.

2. *Special centers.* In most schools, the center of each classroom is the classroom itself. Think about setting up several centers within the room, setting them off from one another with bookcases, movable shelves or partitions, filing cabinets, or furniture. You can also make a center by arranging chairs or desks around a table or carpet. Corners are good places, too, especially in old buildings, which have a lot of them. What may seem like a cramped, dusty nook may, with a little fixing up, be just the place for a student or two to learn best.

Learning centers or stations. Learning centers have tables and seats, bins, files, and shelves for projects and assignments, and typewriters and computers. Students may go there when they have free time, or you may prefer to work out a progression from center to center as part of each student's daily schedule. It helps to have some rules about how many students may be in a center at any one time and what they may and may not do there. In the lower grades, centers can be marked with colored labels—blue for biography and history, yellow for fiction and stories, or blue shelves for in-class projects, red shelves for painting and drawing materials.

Interest centers. Similar to learning centers, interest centers focus on a special interest or theme. One example: the themes of the chapters of the textbook the class is using can form subjects for interest centers.

Carrels. Carrels are walled-in spaces for individual work, each having a chair, a desktop, and a shelf above for books. Some are movable. Carrels give students psychological privacy and increased ability to concentrate right in the classroom. Some schools have carrels left over from the heyday of language labs.

Lofts. Lofts—two-story, roughly made, semiopen rooms—have the appeal of a treehouse all the way through grade 8. In them students may work, read, talk, and relax. Planning and building a loft is a good cooperative project for the class, the shop class, and others in the school.

The teacher's desk. Your desk is probably the most important spot in the room, so you should think about making it easy to talk with you there. Some teachers put a couple of chairs near their desks, partially set off from the rest of the room, where students can talk comfortably. A small table helps, too, if you are going to be looking at written work. A sign-up list on the board keeps students from having to wait in line to see you.

Classroom library. Although the school library is of immense value for teaching and learning, it is not "right there." For some students this is a major obstacle, for others a pleasure. If you can collect some books for your own classroom and work out a simple system for borrowing and returning them, students will do much more reading and looking up than they will if they always have to go to the library. Students may donate books, and the school may have money available for classroom collections. Think about moving some of the books around from time to time to catch attention. For some reason, moving books around stimulates their use. A revolving exhibit of three or four books on the chalk rail works as well as anything.

Book exchange. Students who wish to give books away can be given shelf space. This "barter" economy can may involve some record keeping—which often can be delegated to students—but it stimulates reading, writing, and conversation.

3. *Furniture.* This is not the place for a treatise on classroom furniture, but here are a few suggestions.

A place of one's own. Most students like to have a place they can call their own and where they can store things. There is much to be said for the old-fashioned classroom desk with storage space under the lid. If necessary, lids can be equipped with combination locks, which is much less expensive than having lockers. It should be understood that students' desks or lockers are private. If you believe a student's desk or locker is such a mess that it inhibits learning, or if you suspect that it contains something harmful or undesirable, you should give warning that you need to inspect it and do so in the presence of the student. It should also be understood that your desk is private.

Donated furniture. Don't forget the possibility of donated furniture, if your school does not have regulations against it. A few easy chairs, bureaus, cabinets, a couch or two, and rugs and carpets can often be found among school families or at yard sales, second-hand stores, and rummage sales.

Old school furniture. Explore the basement and storage areas of the school for usable old furniture that has been set aside. The old and worn, which often has far more appeal than the new, can provide variety, stimulation, and comfort.

4. *Signs and labels.* Liberal use of signs is a method of teaching in rooms where children are still learning to read and build their vocabularies. You and the children can print names of places, directions, rules, shelf labels, riddles, quotations, and anything else of interest on large sheets of paper or tagboard and hang them around the room.

5. *Visitors.* Some schools and classes make elaborate preparations for visitors—a map of the room, a sheet explaining what goes on and pointing out features the visitor might look out for—and others do very little. In general, especially in multicenter classrooms in elementary schools, it helps to have a few students who are ready to give visitors a tour of the room and explain what goes on. Some students enjoy doing this, it makes a good impression on visitors, and it lets you keep on with your work without making visitors feel ignored.

The classroom door. Some teachers seem to feel that people will think they have something to hide if they close the door. In most cases, a class does better, and so does the teacher, if the door is closed. There is less distraction from the parade of life in the corridor outside, and the students you teach feel freer to proceed with their work. If the door is closed, it should be understood that visitors—colleagues, supervisors, principal, parents—may, having earlier asked permission, come in and sit down quietly near the back. You may wish to ask them to identify themselves, but it is probably better just to let them watch and listen. It almost never works to try to involve visitors in what is going on.

It helps visitors, as well as new students and teachers, to have every

86

classroom numbered and to have the name of the teacher(s), subject(s), and grade(s) posted outside. Those who are familiar with the school often forget how hard it is for visitors and newcomers to find their way around.

14.
Selecting, Organizing, and Managing the Materials

As teachers, we have considerable influence in selecting, organizing, and managing the materials our students use in our classes. However, in many cases we are given texts and other materials and told, "Here's what the curriculum requires. Use these well," or even, "Use them this way." If we are new to a school, we should do just that. When we become more established, we can take part in getting even better materials and using them better. We should neither crusade from day one nor just placidly accept.

Books

The most valuable "materials" to use for teaching are books—books read and discussed, mastered and enjoyed, related to the experiences and feelings of students. They are also the best sources of vicarious experience; you don't have to *do* everything to learn about it. Further, in this age of devices and machinery, a book is a nearly ideal teaching machine. It is light, portable, attractive, durable, and tough. It covers a vast range of subjects. It is entirely self-pacing, perfect for all teaching methods. And it is cheap, especially if it is a paperback.

These days, it is fashionable to scorn standard hardcover textbooks, which sometimes come in series, last a long time, and often are accompanied by workbooks. Although I will admit that I have never wanted to stick with a series of workbooks for more than two or three years, I believe that a well-organized textbook and its accompaniments are far better than the chaos that results when an inexperienced teacher tries to improvise too much.

Good texts and textbook series are skillfully put together, usually by able teachers and experienced editors. They are geared to individualized instruction, with students moving at their own pace. And many published workbooks and prepared ditto masters contain better exercises than we can devise in the short time most of us have. So don't scorn published materials. Take time at education conferences to visit the exhibits to see new textbooks and workbooks. But don't neglect old books. A good literature anthology, for example, never goes out of date. You and your students can use it year after year.

Many publishing companies now provide a marvelous selection of fairly inexpensive paperbacks. They present them in various ways to stimulate individual interest and initiative while offering enough supporting materials—guidebooks, ditto masters, cassettes, posters—to give sound structure and coherence to a class.

Some hard-pressed teachers worry about using more than one textbook or one system of teaching because they can't possibly read and know all the books they might have in their classrooms that their students might use. This doesn't matter as long as you have a general idea of what is available. There are several points to be made in this connection.

■ The only books you need to read all the way through and know thoroughly are the ones you expect to teach to the entire group or to refer to very often. Students can help you and their classmates by telling about new books they have read and liked. By having students write short reports evaluating the books they read, you can find out what they are reading and how they are reacting to it. You might wish to start a "best books" board, a "highly recommended" file, or, as a reverse twist, a "don't read" list.

■ Another idea is to make up a long list of books for independent reading for the students in your class. Sometimes it helps to divide the list into "hard," "average," and "easy" categories. Many teachers require students to read a certain number of books for the list every two weeks or every month, making allowances for those who simply cannot read that much or are temporarily preoccupied with other concerns.

■ Another way to encourage students to read more is to give them independent reading notebooks in which they may keep a record of the reading they do. Instead of writing the usual dreary full-length book report, they can record author, title, and number of pages, note where they found the book, rate it for difficulty and enjoyment, describe it briefly, and comment on how the book affected them and to whom they would recommend it. This system enables you to evaluate students' reading and to keep in touch with what they are reading so that you can recommend books to others.

Other materials

Here are some suggestions for materials other than books that can be used in the classroom.

Miscellaneous materials. For lower grades, collect cardboard for word games, paper bags for drawing masks, old socks in which to put things to be felt but not seen and then written about, spring clips for hanging exhibit items to be talked and written about, and so on, and on.

Charts. Post large charts around the upper reaches of the room giving frequently needed information. In an English class, charts can give the approved form for writing papers and assignments, grammar symbols, principal rules of spelling and punctuation, characteristics of short stories. Similar charts can be made for mathematics, science, and social studies. Having information always visible in the room means that it is right there when the students need it, and they can use it without help from anyone else. A chart also enables you to refer to a needed item without having to search through a book for it.

Individual student folders. It is useful to keep folders for individual students in which you, or preferably they, file everything they have produced at home or in class after you have dealt with it. You can use this material to show students their progress and accomplishments as well as areas in which they need to improve. If you post a list of each paper and assignment that students are supposed to have done, they can check their folders to be sure that everything that should be there is there.

Computers

Computers are here to stay. They won't bring utopia, and they won't lead us away from the basics of reading, writing, reckoning, and reasoning, but, if properly used, they can help students in all these areas. And, since computers are here to stay, we and our students should learn how to use them and keep abreast of their development. If we don't, we will soon be out of touch with our students. If our students don't, they will be out of touch with the world they are growing into.

"Computer awareness" can start early. In kindergarten and the early grades, children can learn about the keyboard and see things happen on the screen by playing games. Then they can learn how to use a computer to perform specific tasks. By the time they graduate from school, and preferably before, they should know how to touch-type, how to use a word processor, and how to retrieve information stored in or accessible by a computer. In short, they should know how to use a computer as a drill-master, tutor, and teacher. At the same time, they should have chances to talk about the effects of computers on society.

Teachers should become computer literate, too, and keep their eyes open to the various uses that can be—and are being—made of the computer throughout the school. At the same time, we must remember that nothing can replace classroom discussion in which students, guided by teachers, exchange ideas about important questions and stimulate and advance one another's understanding.

Although the computer can meet the needs of some students for advanced original independent work and teach them efficiently and well beyond the knowledge of most regular teachers, we must be sure that it does not cut off or separate these students from the activities and interests of their classmates.

Finally, we will have to learn for ourselves how best to deal with new excuses for failing to do assignments—no longer "The dog ate my homework," but, now, "The computer erased my disk."

Special materials

Learning and stimulation can be increased if the classroom is equipped with certain items, provided they are affordable.

Typewriters. A couple of typewriters are a valuable addition to any classroom. Students can teach themselves to touch-type on a typewriter or computer keyboard.

Overhead projector and screen. By keeping an overhead projector and screen always in the same place so that you may use them quickly, you can concentrate the attention of the class on a single point as you deal with a paper, an item in a book, a drawing, or a handmade transparency. The chalkboard is more reliable, and has no bulb to burn out, but the projector is an excellent supplement.

Tape recorder. This device can stimulate learning in several ways. Students can record and play back to the class a passage, sound effect, or skit as a stimulus for discussion. Recordings of words, music, or both sometimes move students in ways that your voice and theirs cannot. Students who simply cannot get started writing are sometimes helped by talking into a tape recorder and then playing back and copying what they said. You can tape a special assignment in advance for students, who then listen to the instructions and follow them. (It is strange how sometimes our electronic voice can compel more concentrated attention than our live voice.)

Video equipment. Video equipment, more sophisticated and expensive than a tape recorder, provides immediate sight and sound feedback, all the way from what has just happened to a galaxy of readily available performances and demonstrations on cassette. If the class has just read a scene from *Romeo and Juliet,* for example, seeing the same scene acted by the Royal Shakespeare Company is a superb way to deepen understanding and enjoyment. Video can also be used to help you evaluate your own teaching, to show a PTA meeting exactly what is going on in classes, to help a dance team see how well they are working together. In addition to letting us see ourselves as others see us, video can bring a large part of the world into the classroom, on demand. We must guard against becoming so fascinated with it that it dominates classroom time and attention.

Calendar, maps. A large calendar is an item some classrooms don't have and should. Even more important are two large maps — one of the world, preferably with the United States shown somewhere other than at the center, and one of the United States. A detailed map of the school's community is also useful. Like the calendar, maps are a constant source of reality, stimulation, and orientation to the world. Even more valuable are two sets of maps, one showing only the physical features of the earth, the nation, and the community, and the other set showing only political features. And having large photographs of earth taken from spaceships teaches the valuable lesson that national boundaries are not visible from space.

Curtain or large folding screen. Curtains and screens are both easy to make and are not expensive. Though not essential, they are useful for skits, acting short scenes of plays, and for sound- and voice-only effects.

Lectern. Anyone who makes speeches knows how convenient it is to have someplace to put your notes, but thousands of students are required to read papers, deliver speeches, and make reports from papers and notes held in shaking hands or put on a table or desk. A solid music stand works well and is adjustable. The real world provides lecterns for speakers, so why not the classroom?

Soon after they settle in at a new school, teachers should find out what they need to do to procure equipment and materials to improve their work and their classrooms.

Television

Television is a material that is impossible to "select, organize, and manage," except when videos are involved. Its influence in your classroom weighs heavily, and it is largely out of your control. In America, the average home television set is on six and a half hours a day; preschoolers watch thirty to fifty hours a week, spending more than a third of their waking hours before the screen. By graduation, the average high school student will have viewed 18,000 hours of television but experienced only 11,000 hours of classroom instruction. The average American high school student averages four hours of homework a week and thirty hours of television.

It is a major point that the damaging effects of television grow out of the process of watching it, not out of the poor content of programs. In

The Plug-In Drug (New York: Bantam, 1978), Marie Winn quotes a mother: "My five-year-old goes into a trance when he watches TV. He just gets locked into what is happening on the screen. He's totally, absolutely absorbed when he watches and oblivious to anything else. If I speak to him when he's watching TV he absolutely doesn't hear me. To get his attention I have to turn the set off. Then he snaps out of it."

Watching television for long periods of time is damaging because the programs move at their own fast pace, allowing no time for pause or reflection, no interaction with other minds, no participation, only passive receiving of mind-monopolizing stimuli. Television walls its viewers off from family and friends; it can cripple social competence and the ability to discuss, to challenge, or to relate to others intellectually—or in any way except by physical proximity. Its images keep shifting, its content comes in vivid visual splashes reinforced by music, sound effects, and voices, and it totally lacks the left-to-right sequentiality that reading requires.

Defenders of television point out that viewers hear hours of standard English most of the time (not necessarily so) and that they receive vast amounts of information and vividly experience worlds they would otherwise never know. However, they have no chance to *use* the standard English, or to *cope* with the information, or to *react* to the worlds—that is, to think about what they view. A headline in the London *Times,* above an article on the effects of American television on Great Britain, read, "They Came, We Saw, They Conquered." The article told how happily and willingly the British were "conquered." No resistance to the pleasure, according to the author. The same can happen anywhere.

So how should we in our classrooms try to manage television and its effects? Do we condemn it to our students and ban it from the premises and the activities we preside over? Or do we accept it as an inevitable competitor and try to turn it into an ally?

■ Mere condemnation can only harm the education of real television addicts. Television has become so much a part of their personalities and process of thinking and perceiving that to condemn it is, to a considerable extent, to condemn them as people—and ourselves as irrelevant. It's something like rejecting all English that is not standard English. Condemn children's language or their deeply established habits and they feel themselves condemned, lessened, and antagonized.

■ Instead of condemning television, try to exploit its educational advantages, and, by showing how books and talk can be even better, wean students from depending on television. If they come from families in which books, conversation, and thought are highly valued, weaning them from television may be easy and the families will be grateful for your support. Most families believe in reading and conversation, even though they may not practice what they believe.

■ Sometimes programs do come along whose content is so valuable and in which the visual experience is so important—probing reports on community and world situations, debates on contemporary or enduring issues, science demonstrations, travel experiences, real plays genuinely acted—that you and your students, by experiencing them in common, can use them to stimulate classroom discussion and, later, reading and writing. These programs can be videotaped so that you may use them at the best moment.

■ Show students that a picture on television is not the whole truth; it's inevitably edited—probably more than an account in the newspaper. If the class compares the two, they will probably find that television must zip urgently from happening to happening, and vivid though a picture may be, and convincing as it may seem, it is inevitably only a slice of the whole and therefore incomplete. An interesting exercise is to have students do a videotaped "report" of a class, editing the forty-five minutes down to ten—which amounts to much less cutting than the typical television news event gets. The class can view the report and discuss how accurately it depicts what actually took place.

■ Don't be afraid to prescribe television time-off on school nights, when homework must be done and books read. Explain clearly to parents the reason for your prescription—which will be stronger if you can get the school's administration or your academic department to administer it rather than having to do this yourself.

■ Now and then, to stay in touch with the lives of your students, you need to experience some of their favorite programs yourself, eye to tube. Take some time to do this.

Cleanup and maintenance

Whenever we use a place or thing, we should try to leave it in as good condition as we found it or better. Through class discussion, students can be brought to see the advantage to all if each person does his or her share of the "housekeeping." Tasks can be distributed according to preference and skill, but the aim should be shared responsibility. Tasks can range all the way from erasing the board to operating the video equipment and editing tapes.

Doing one's share offers many opportunities for modest glory and self-esteem. Often those who are not the most fluent readers, the best speakers, or the most creative poster makers become the best projectionists, book shelvers, and bulletin board arrangers.

It is worth spending class time on developing proper attitudes toward this aspect of school life. Avoid the attitude that says "Let the janitor take care of it. After all, it's his job, and we have more important things to do."

And don't assume that all the nice, pleasant ways of organizing that work with young children will not work with adolescents, too. Schools tend to slide into sloppiness as students get up into seventh and eighth grade, probably because teachers become more exclusively concerned with academic work and discipline. These will go better if concern for orderliness continues, not by fiat, but through discussion, agreement, and commitment.

If possible, try to get this movement going early in the year instead of waiting until things go to pot or you get angry because you have to do it all yourself. Remember, a martyr is someone who has to live with a saint, and we should not expect our students to be martyrs.

15.

Organizing the Time

In Ingmar Bergman's movie *Scenes from a Marriage,* Marianne says, "Just think about it. Our life's mapped out into little squares—every day, every hour, every minute. The squares are filled, one by one, and in good time. If there's suddenly an empty square, we're dismayed."

So it is in most schools, even more than in other parts of life.

The master schedule

Almost any class, especially a self-contained one, benefits from having the basic schedule for the day written on the board or in some other place where all can see and work from it. This schedule provides the spine for the day's work.

Once students are out of elementary school, however, and they study different subjects at different times, the schedule too often becomes king, security blanket, welcome scapegoat, excuse for not thinking. Yet we obviously must have schedules to enable teachers and students to plan ahead and to experience each day the regularity and routine that a schedule provides. We all need some of that security, even though we all should, on occasion, be dismayed and challenged by "suddenly an empty square."

In 1942, the Eight-Year Study of the Progressive Education Association reported on its experiment with some thirty schools that considered themselves and had been chosen as "progressive." As a part of the experiment, the schools had been liberated, for eight years in the 1930's, from the college-imposed curriculum requirements against which many of them had been protesting. What happened in some of them was not much, which led the authors of the report to remark, "We have grown to love our chains."

We do indeed grow to love, because we genuinely need them, time blocks within which we can do our work. But the schedule should respond to the educational program, never determine or limit it. We must never be afraid to ask the schedule maker, for whom a neat, nicely working time plan can become a piece of addictive beauty disembodied from its vital purpose, to let up and think flexibly. Fortunately, the computer makes flexible thinking and change easier to adopt or adapt to.

We should start with the best educational program we can devise and then see if it can be scheduled. But most of us are no good at making schedules. We are much better at seeing all too narrowly and defending passionately our own needs only. In making a schedule—no matter how sophisticated the technique—everyone has to give in order to get a schedule that is best for the whole school.

Using time out of school

One way or another, children are being educated and miseducated, in and out of school, all the time, and there is no switch for turning a mind off or on. Here are some thoughts about the time out of school.

Some students and their parents feel that weekends should be kept inviolate, uninvaded by required schoolwork. This view is educationally invalid. If what is happening at school has any meaning or momentum, then weekends are going to be important, thick slices of time when students can work on their own. We should not, however, be so impressed with our own assignments that we can't appreciate the benefits that many students derive from weekends away from all thoughts of school—pursuing their own interests, taking off with friends, or just doing nothing. We should assign homework far enough ahead to let students plan time for nonschool activities.

The four-day week has become a reality in some places. Most school people do not question the value of three months off in the summer, even though the original reason for it—work on the farm—no longer exists in most places. But the five-day school week is still almost universal, if only because it coincides with the five-day work week. When, a few years ago, some schools in Maine switched to a four-day week to save fuel, people were surprised to find that students learned as well or better than they had done during the same number of five-day weeks. A lot of intelligent planning was involved, of course, but the lesson here is that we should not live unexamined lives and that different plans may work better than our usual ones.

Another path to free time

Many schools where students do not have to be under direct supervision all the time allow students to use their free time as they wish when no class is scheduled.

Some schools let students go wherever they want, even (with written parental permission) off campus, provided they attend all classes and other scheduled events, such as homeroom periods and assemblies. The grade level at which such freedom can be used beneficially depends on what goes on out of and around the school. Usually, this kind of free time is the privilege only of high school juniors and seniors.

Students need to understand that this freedom is granted only to those who make proper use of it, maintain a satisfactory record, stay out of trouble, and meet scheduled obligations. They must also understand that this privilege may be withdrawn or restricted if the freedom is not used in ways that are acceptable to the community.

When it becomes necessary to restrict this freedom, it is usually best to do it for a specific period of time or until a definite goal—finishing a paper, achieving a certain level of skill, changing behavior—is reached. It is probably better for the student's guidance counselor, homeroom teacher, or grade head to do the restricting than to have just any teacher "slap the kid into study hall" for the rest of the year. Be sure to allow for some consideration and reflection—fairness—before taking drastic action.

More ideas about time

The following suggestions can prove as successful as they are simple. They work.

■ Have a large clock in each classroom, starting in nursery school. If you are the only one wearing a watch, and only a bell marks the ends of periods, students miss out on a constant low-key opportunity to adjust to the real demands of time. Clocks do not strengthen the tyranny of time; rather, they oblige time to show its face so that it can be dealt with as a reality, out in the open, instead of being hidden until, at the bell, it jumps out at student and teacher alike. Experienced teachers in conventional schools are always aware of what time it is—time of day, and how far into the period they are—and adjust their plans accordingly. Students, too, should be aware of the time and make judgments accordingly.

■ Post your schedule and an appointment sign-up sheet in a place where everyone can see at a glance when you are and are not available, with free periods clearly marked. You can have the sign-up sheet in the room or outside the door, in case you're teaching, for students who need to see you during or after school.

16.
Evaluating and Testing the Performance of Students

A *New Yorker* drawing by Whitney Darrow shows a nasty-looking little boy and his puzzled mother in the office of the school counselor, who is saying confidently, "Mrs. Minton, there's no such thing as a bad boy. Hostile, perhaps. Aggressive, recalcitrant, even sadistic. But not *bad*."

This is the truth: we find bad performance, bad behavior, bad attitudes, bad feelings—but not bad girls or boys. Whenever we are called upon to evaluate, our job is to describe, as objectively as we can, the academic performance and school behavior of our students. We are not there to evaluate them as people.

What should teachers evaluate?

We are on the soundest ground if we stick to testing and evaluating the academic skills and knowledge of our students. However, as we consider their work and progress, we should not separate schoolwork from other behavior, because "nonacademic" behavior often helps to explain academic performance, good and bad.

Our students' feelings and behavior affect how well they can learn. We should note at the end of each day those who are having difficulty or causing trouble. We should know who seems troubled, who acts nervous, who sulks, who never talks, who is "hostile, aggressive, recalcitrant, even sadistic," and when and how (but probably not why, because we are not psychiatrists). We should also know who seems friendly, healthily competitive, cooperative, and even altruistic.

Many schools seek to help students develop sound values: democratic, religious, moral, or humanistic. We are never justified in marking or grading students on their values, but we may wish to be ready with opinions, comments, or even ratings on aspects of "citizenship." Citizenship in schools is usually defined as assuming responsibility, cooperating, developing and obeying rules, respecting property, working and playing well with others, being courteous, and "work habits" — making good use of time and materials, doing thorough and careful work, completing assignments on time, putting forth effort.

The primary job of evaluation, however, is in testing and measuring academic skills and knowledge of subject matter.

Why test?

The purpose of testing should be to obtain useful data. It is foolish to give more tests than are needed, spending time and money on results that are filed for later use, "just in case." Test data can be used (1) to give teachers information to use in planning for and with each student and each class, (2) to inform students and their teachers how well they are doing, where their strengths and weaknesses lie, and what they need to do about them, (3) to inform parents about the academic progress of their children, (4) to suggest to the school how well it is developing skills and teaching subject matter and to indicate needed changes, (5) to help decide, and communicate to parents, where a student should be placed in school, (6) to give schools, colleges, and professional schools some idea whether students are likely to do well if admitted, and (7) to tell the community how well its school or schools are doing, both in the academic accomplishment of their students and in comparison with schools across the state and the nation.

Some testing terms

Here are some basic terms and concepts that all teachers should know if they are to make and use tests intelligently.

Valid and invalid tests. The first thing to consider about any test is its validity: whether it tests what it is supposed to test. For example, a paper-and-pencil test consisting of ten simple subtraction problems, with no time limit, stands a good chance of being a valid test of the ability to subtract using pencil and paper. But a three-minute test consisting of twenty-five such problems, each involving two long numbers, is a test not only of ability to subtract but also of speed and keeping cool under pressure. Teachers are not always aware of the many reasons why tests may be invalid. Here are three examples.

■ A sophomore always scored in the high 90's in a college economics course for which she didn't do much of the reading because she was able to tell which answers on long multiple-choice tests sounded right. So she was an expert in reading the professor's mind, not in economics.

■ A language study showed that children in a Pittsburgh ghetto, as part of their daily speech, used some 3,800 words, expressions, and constructions that did not appear in dictionaries and grammars of standard English. Tests of standard English were therefore invalid measures of the language ability of these children because the children did not habitually use most of the vocabulary of the tests.

■ According to one study, the College Board's Scholastic Aptitude Test is a valid predictor of a student's ability to succeed (that is, to get good grades in college) but an invalid test of likely later success and satisfaction in the professions — medicine, architecture, education, law. According to other studies, a better predictor of success and satisfaction in life after college is a complete and accurate list of achievement in extracurricular activities in school and college.

Reliable and unreliable tests. A reliable test is one that yields consistent results when repeated. For example, designers of IQ tests conduct careful studies to see whether individual children tend to obtain similar scores when retested at different ages. Reliable results in teacher-made tests are produced by giving tests under uniform conditions each time. They should also contain a broad sampling of the content or skills being tested. Unreliable tests might include a five-item true-false test on a long unit in which students of equal knowledge could score very differently, or tests given just before lunch, or just after a fight, or tests in which the questions are quickly read aloud once or written illegibly on the board.

Objective tests. Many teachers feel that if a test has lots of items, and if each item has a correct answer, and if the whole thing adds up to a definite score, it is an objective test. It is, in the sense that the score is not affected by the test scorer's attitude toward the person being tested, the handwriting on the test, or how the person making the test is feeling that day. The test may not be objective in the usual sense of the word, however, if test items tend to favor a particular type of student, or if things other than knowledge or skills — like students' ability to make intelligent guesses or inability to understand the question format — affect the results. A single, well-constructed essay question or a series of carefully composed brief-answer questions may actually, if read and graded skillfully, be more objective than a long series of test items that produce a score.

Raw score. In any test, the number of items the student gets right is the raw score. The raw score has little meaning until it is compared with raw scores of other students. This comparison is commonly expressed as a standard score, a percentile, or a grade equivalent (see below).

Norm. A norm is simply a standard against which to compare the performance of an individual or class. Published norms for widely used tests are usually based on the performance of public school pupils across the nation. For schools that are highly selective, these norms are often not very helpful because so many of their students cluster near the top of the scale.

Types of tests

Standardized or norm-referenced test. A standardized or norm-referenced test is one that has been tried out on a large number of students to establish a standard of performance, or norm, by grade or age level on the various sections of the test. Most tests published by large companies are standardized to enable schools to compare the performance of their students with that of the "average" student of the same age and, to some extent, the same background. By contrast, a teacher-made test is not standardized, except against a standard that the teacher may have established mentally or on the basis of experience with the test over several years.

Criterion-referenced test. In a criterion-referenced test, students' scores are compared with a fixed standard of achievement, not with the performance of other students. For example, a school might decide that the criterion for promotion to the next grade or a new unit is 80 per cent correct answers on a given reading comprehension, biology, history, or mathematics test. Students who reach 80 per cent are promoted. Those failing to reach this criterion are given additional instruction until they score 80 per cent. Criterion-referenced tests are useful in evaluating the achievement of one individual according to particular goals set for that student.

Aptitude test. This test supposedly measures aptitude for certain academic or other work, not actual achievement in the field. A well-known aptitude test is the College Board's Scholastic Aptitude Test, which is widely used to measure aptitude for college work. The SAT is scored in a scale of 200-800, with 500 the median (middle) score, based on comparison with others bound for college. The SAT yields a verbal score, a mathematical score, and a total score. A person who scores 675 on the verbal section, 730 on math, a total of 1,405, *probably* has a high aptitude for college work. One who scores V 325, M 310, total 635, *probably* has low aptitude. However, such is life, and such are tests, that some 650-score people do well in college and some 1,400-score ones do not. Another widely used test of achievement and aptitude is the American College Testing Program Assessment (ACT).

Intelligence test. An intelligence test is a special kind of aptitude test that measures "intelligence," whatever that may be. Whether or not intelligence, or intelligences, can be measured is still an unsettled question. Most people, perhaps especially teachers, tend to define intelligence as something that can be measured by an IQ test, but it is important to remind ourselves that "intelligence" is a complicated set of concepts. In actuality, human beings demonstrate a number of intelligences. Howard Gardner has described seven of these in *Frames of Mind: The Theory of Multiple Intelligences* (New York: Basic Books, 1983) as linguistic, musical, logical-mathematical, spatial, bodily-kinesthetic, and the personal intelligences (intrapersonal — "access to one's feeling life" — and interpersonal). As we "instruct," we must be aware that we are directly and purposefully dealing with only some of the intelligences of our students, no matter what their age. Moreover, we should keep in mind that some people perform some mental tasks better than others, such as recall and memory, reasoning, defining, using numbers, solving problems — the kinds of things that one is likely to be asked to do in school.

An intelligence test determines a person's ability to do mental tasks compared with others of a given age. Child A, ten years old, has a mental age scored at fourteen and thus has a higher intelligence score than Child B, also ten, but whose mental age is nine. The score is given as an intelligence quotient, or IQ, the result of dividing the mental age by the chronological age.

Child A   MA 14/CA 10 = IQ 140
Child B   MA 9/CA 10 = IQ 90

Theoretically, the average intelligence score is 100, meaning that the average person's mental and chronological ages are the same. The range for average intelligence is 90-110; scores above 130 or below 70 are highly unusual.

Everyone acknowledges that many difficult, perhaps impossible, problems are connected with measuring intelligence. Test makers try to use items to which everyone tested has had the same exposure, but every IQ test is to some degree a measure of experience.

People do poorly on IQ tests for many reasons. Perhaps the test is in English, and the child taking it speaks mostly Spanish, or the child is sick, afraid, missed breakfast, or is worried about something that is going on at home. Thus it is important for us to say "IQ *score*," not just "IQ," to avoid making an absolute statement about intelligence. This is far from saying that IQ tests are of no value, however. Some tend to be good predictors of success in school and may provide important information for use in educational planning.

Most schools give fairly short IQ tests, administered to a group, that rely on the ability to read and, in some cases, to listen. These group tests, inexpensive and easy to score, are much less valid and reliable than individually administered tests. A much better but more expensive example of an individually administered test is the Wechsler Intelligence Scale for Children-Revised (WISC-R). This test does not rely on reading ability and provides several subscores that allow the experienced test giver to analyze a child's profile of mental abilities. If a school can afford it, all children should be given an individual IQ test as a diagnostic measure to help in understanding their style of learning and in planning teaching strategies. If individual testing for everyone is too expensive, then those children who seem to be having academic problems should take the WISC-

R or newer alternatives, such as the revised Stanford-Binet or Kaufman ABC as an early step in diagnosis. Maybe they have genuinely low academic intelligence and will need special support in school. If they have been doing poorly, however, and score well overall on some subtests, further study and diagnosis are called for.

Many parents, and some teachers, tend to see IQ scores as tremendously significant, almost magic numbers that can be used to compare children with one another and with other people's children. Others believe that IQ scores don't mean a thing. Clearly, IQ scores, if given to parents or teachers, should always be accompanied by careful interpretation.

Achievement test. An achievement test differs from an aptitude or an intelligence test in that it measures information acquired and skills developed in specific subjects taught in school, not general knowledge. Achievement tests are useful for discovering whether students have learned what the test measures—which may or may not be what their teachers set out to teach them. The best of these tests are made up after careful study of what students in American schools are supposed to know, and they are revised from time to time to keep them up with changes in the curriculum. The College Board's achievement tests are widely used as a measure of knowledge of subject matter in connection with admission to college, as are the ACT tests.

Test-taking problems

Other things being equal, people who have had lots of practice taking tests are likely to do better on them than those who have not. Good published tests always start with practice items with directions read aloud. Some students have real difficulties with the mechanics of taking tests—circling answers, keeping track of the right place on a separate answer sheet—which have absolutely no connection with the subject matter or skill being tested. So, when a student gets a low score on a test but is doing perfectly well in the schoolwork being tested, we should be skeptical about this low score and perhaps go over the test items with the student. Chapters 17 and 18 give some suggestions about helping students take standardized and teacher-made tests and examinations.

Some teachers give better marks to students who score well on standardized tests than to those who perform equally well in school but whose test scores are low. It is important for teachers to use test scores as *information* to help them plan with students for assignments, reading, course choices, and other work. It is equally important for teachers to evaluate students' actual work without reference to standardized test scores.

Some final points

■ Perhaps our society and our schools rely too much on tests. A score is so much easier to deal with than a complex human being. Even so, we do need tests administered to groups, for we don't have time to examine each student's performance individually.

■ If a student is having great difficulty in performing well at school, whether in academic subjects and skills or in other ways, and if we have worked hard to help the student do better, a part of the school's evaluation and testing should probably involve referring the student to a counselor for an evaluation and for suggestions about how the school and parents can help. Teachers should know what sources of psychological testing, evaluation, and counseling are available and consult someone in the school — guidance counselor, principal, supervisor, homeroom teacher — when help seems needed. Care and tact should be used in talking about or suggesting counseling or evaluation to parents and students. In some cases, it is probably better for someone other than the teacher who identifies the need to initiate this kind of conversation.

Some people believe that children who have problems need special attention and protection from the fierce world. In fact, what psychologists and psychiatrists most often recommend for students with adjustment problems is more exposure to healthy reality, not less. They may also need special remedial work or counseling. Better than saying, "Here's a problem kid. I've got to go easy," is dealing objectively and realistically with that student.

■ In observing and evaluating the performance of students, always remember how varied they are. Pay attention to surface clues, but remember how little of people shows on the surface. And don't let yourself think you're looking into a mirror when you look at a student. When they look a certain way it doesn't mean that inside they are the way you are when you look that way.

108

17.

Using and Misusing Standardized Tests

There is no question that standardized tests can be used by schools and teachers in ways that are harmful to students. Tests may use one kind of language, the student another; some bright children are poor test takers; some test items seem to penalize the extra bright, who see things in them that the item writers did not see. Sometimes students get low scores firmly stuck on them, so they think they're dumb, their parents and teachers treat them as if they were dumb, and they naturally develop feelings of inferiority and discouragement. The result is, to use Jonathan Kozol's phrase, "death at an early age."

Avoiding the bad effects of tests

Tests do not need to be used in negative ways. Here are some suggestions for avoiding educational disasters.

■ Never use a test score or set of scores as the sole criterion for judging the performance of students or estimating their potential performance. Test scores should be considered one piece of information that is be used in conjunction with a lot of other information.

■ If some students get low test scores but perform well in their schoolwork, try to find out what the testing difficulty is and help them overcome it.

■ In telling students or their parents what their standardized test or IQ scores are, explain carefully the basis and limited importance of these numbers.

■ Use test scores mainly as a diagnostic tool to help plan students' work and the materials you use to teach classes.

■ If a student makes a very low score on a group intelligence test, try to get the school to give an individually administered test before deciding that the student's academic intelligence is low.

■ Remember, on any properly normed standardized test, half of all the students who take it, not just the ones in your school, will inevitably score at the middle or below, and half at the middle or above. You may have more students in the bottom or the top half, but this in itself is not a sufficient basis for judging the quality of teaching in the school. (See more on this in Chapter 23.)

■ If you teach in a school that admits only bright college-bound students and the school uses so-called "independent school norms," remember that testing below the 50th percentile does not mean "below average" in comparison to the population as a whole.

■ If you think it might help, use test scores to encourage students, but never to shame or discourage them. *Never* compare the test scores of students in public.

Typical standardized tests

Over the years, I have examined the administrative procedures and content of many widely used standardized achievement tests. I have also worked as a "subject matter expert" in constructing multiple-choice items for one of the most reputable, careful, and conscientious test publishers, and may therefore be somewhat biased on their favor. I believe that the major published tests are useful instruments but that they have limited purposes and should be held firmly within their complicated educational context.

Before describing a typical test, I should explain how the content is selected. A careful survey is made of the curriculum and materials of large numbers of schools across the country, and test items are based on the content that is most commonly found in them. Obviously, to the extent that teachers teach for the tests, this process has a tendency to push education toward a central core. If a school believes itself to be on a fringe—and there are some excellent fringes—it should make allowances for this as it considers testing and test results.

Given the criticisms of multiple-choice items, you might think that they are put together capriciously or carelessly, but the facts are otherwise. From the selected body of content, teams of item writers make up items and then try them out on two or three other item writers to catch those that don't work—for example, they can't agree on what the correct answer is, or they find that certain words or language are misleading. Such items are cut or reconstructed and retried.

Then the items are put together and tried out in several classrooms to see which ones work. When an "item analysis" of the test is made, it turns out that everyone "gets" some items (of no use for this kind of test) and that everyone misses others (also of no use). With some other items, the people who do well on the entire test are more likely to get wrong answers than people who do poorly; because of their surprise reverse twist, these items are discarded.

After this process is completed, a test made up of items shown by actual experience to work well with most groups most of the time can be constructed. They do a pretty good job of measuring a student's knowledge and achievement in the areas they claim to test—provided the students have been living in more or less "typical" homes and have been through a more or less typical American school curriculum.

An all-school testing program

It is educationally sound for a school or school system each year to give all students, starting about third grade, the sections of a recognized standardized test series that measure word-analysis skills, vocabulary and reading comprehension, mathematical reasoning, concepts, and applications, and "language." This kind of testing tends to counteract wishful thinking about how a school population is doing, or even how individual students are doing. It requires us to compare the performance with national norms. It is far less important to have a standardized measure of individual course subject-matter content, which does and should vary from school to school and from class to class.

For students who may be bound for college, a school might switch in grades 9-12 to the tests especially designed to measure what the colleges expect—either the College Board's Scholastic Aptitude and Achievement tests or the American College Testing Program Assessment (ACT). Students should take the preliminary forms, such as the PSAT, as well as the final forms of these tests.

About college tests

If you are a high school teacher, you should be familiar with the aptitude and achievement tests of the College Board and the American College Testing Program. My conviction, based on some careful studies made by the College Board and other more objective authorities, and despite the claims of the proprietors of special test-preparation programs, is that the best preparation for College Board tests and others like them is long exposure to words, reading, writing, ideas, challenges, discussion, and enthusiasm for learning. In the words of the College Board itself, "Generally, the soundest preparation for the SAT is to study widely with emphasis on academic courses and extensive outside reading." Likewise, the College Board achievement tests require solid subject-matter knowledge.

Commercial test-preparation courses are expensive and may take up to ten weeks They are not educational in any but the narrowest sense and may even increase tension and nervousness about the tests. People disagree about whether they increase scores significantly enough to make a difference in how likely students are to be accepted by the college or university of their choice.

Barring disastrously low test scores, more important to colleges in deciding whether to admit students are their high school record (not just marks but also choice of courses), the impression they make in an admission interview, the evidence they present of creativity, independence, concern for others, enthusiasm, initiative, and evidence of outside activities and interests.

Thus schools may wish to discourage parents from enrolling their children in special commercial courses. On the other hand, the school can help by providing times when an expert teacher goes over test information and practice items with students, not leaving it to chance that all students will do a thorough enough job of reading about tests and learning test-taking skills.

Preparing for standardized tests

Teaching students to do as well as they can on tests is quite different from teaching *for* a test. Teaching *how* to take tests can be a legitimate and useful exercise. One of the very best teachers is simply experience in taking tests.

Even though most standardized tests give clear enough directions and a few carefully devised practice items, many students encounter difficulties that have little to do with their knowledge of the subject matter or with the skills supposedly being tested, and thus may need help.

I say "may" need help. It is only honest to point out that in teaching your students how to take these tests you are giving them a certain advantage over the students whose performances were originally used in establishing the standards for the tests. Thus you may be inflating the scores—and grade equivalents and percentiles—of your students and making their performance—and your teaching—look better than it really is. Do you want to do that?

Here, for better or worse, are ways to help students do well on standardized tests.

■ Give them facsimile answer sheets on which they can practice marking their answers, just to see how the system works.

■ Read the directions for the test to the students a day or so in advance so that they will be familiar with them.

■ Duplicate some easy questions in exactly the same form as those on the actual test and let students practice on these, just to get the idea. This exercise will also help them to manage the test booklet, the answer sheet, the pencil, and the operations that require good eye-hand coordination.

■ If students are not penalized for guessing on a particular test (if the score is simply the number correct—the raw score), tell them to spend the last moments quickly filling in all the items they have not yet completed.

■ Tell students to work as fast as they can without being careless and never to puzzle a long time over an item but to come back to it if there is time.

■ Give students two soft, dull pencils each and tell them to make one clear mark in the answer space instead of wasting time neatly filling in circles or spaces.

■ Be sure that students understand the difference between a test situation and a cooperative learning situation, in which working with other students is encouraged as an excellent way to learn. In some schools, especially with younger children, the practice of learning together is so ingrained that students have a hard time switching to a situation in which their individual performance is being measured. A clear explanation and a chance to discuss the reasons for individual testing usually enable people to adjust to a test situation.

Of course, no amount of test-taking practice can compensate for unmastered content.

18.

Making and Grading Your Own Tests

Most school testing consists of teacher-made quizzes, true-false tests, multiple-choice tests, and examinations. The main advantage of teacher-made tests is that they test whether what has been taught has been learned. The main disadvantage, especially for teachers of limited experience, is that such tests give few clues to how well students are doing compared to how well they should be doing, in relation both to their own abilities and to what is normally expected of students of the same age and grade. Teacher-made tests can also be far too "tough" and discouraging, especially if a teacher relishes a reputation as being a "hard" teacher.

On the other hand, a teacher who is anxious to please, too concerned about the supposed fragility and sensitivity of students, and not willing to risk overchallenging pupils may give tests that are far too easy and unrealistically encouraging, which can lead to unrealistic planning on the part of students who are given artificially high grades.

Types of teacher-made tests

Multiple-choice tests. Although they take a lot of time and care to make up, multiple-choice tests can save hours in evaluating how well students have mastered a broad area of subject matter and how soundly they are able to think about it. If you are likely to be teaching the same body of subject matter—a book, a period of history, a science unit—to several sections or for more than one year and plan to use the same teaching materials, it is worth taking the time to devise a good multiple-choice test that covers it. Here are some suggestions on how to go about it.

115

■ Be sure that the reading level of the test items is not beyond any of your students. The test is of the subject, not of the overall ability to read.

■ When you have made a first draft, try it out on someone who knows the subject to see whether any items are misleading and revise the ones that are.

■ Be careful that "wrong" answers, sometimes called "distractors," *sound* as correct as the "right" one. Some words, like "never" and "always," tip savvy test takers off to a "wrong" answer.

■ Be careful not to make your "right" answers consistently longer and more carefully qualified than your "wrong" ones.

■ Here and there, throw in an answer that is so clearly "wrong" that it is funny. This can do wonders for class morale.

■ Avoid trick questions.

■ A duplicated test is far better than one that is read aloud. A duplicated answer sheet also makes life easier for all concerned.

■ One trouble with most multiple-choice tests is that they have three "wrong" answers and one "right" one, thus bombarding students with a fair amount of incorrect information, some of which they may "learn," consciously or unconsciously, while taking the test. Try putting some of the items thus: "All but *one* of the following statements are true. Cross out the one that is false."

■ To be sure that students understand how to do the test and use the answer sheet, give them a couple of practice items that do not count— especially important with "cross out the one that is false" types of items.

■ After correcting the tests, analyze the answers and discuss with the class any questions that most people missed.

True-false tests. These are not much use because it is hard to find items that require more than superficial understanding and yet are not misleading. Especially bad are short true-false tests (fifteen to twenty items) that count heavily in judging a student's work. But short true-false tests do lead nicely into discussion of a subject after students have puzzled over each item. Tests used thus should not be marked, just scored.

Short-answer tests. A useful, simple test is one that asks a question or two and allows students ten to fifteen minutes to write. Make sure your questions are clear and that they cannot be answered just "Yes" or "No" or in a single sentence. Ending questions with "Why?" or "Explain" usually works well.

Examinations. These longer tests cover the work of a semester or an entire year. It is sensible to consider, and to let students know you do, that an examination is not mainly a hurdle to be got over or a hardship to be endured but rather an opportunity for students to show how much they know and how clearly they can think, organize, and write. Preparing for and taking an exam (see below) can and should be part of learning. Here are some suggestions for making, giving, and marking exams.

■ Two- and three-hour exams do not work well for most students in junior high school and below. They do better with short exams or parts of exams.

■ A typical exam is made up of several questions or sections of various types, such as multiple-choice, short-answer, and a longer essay question or two. You can allow students some choice—"Answer any three of the following five questions," for example—but some authorities object to this practice because all students are not tested in the same way on the same material.

■ Indicate on the exam how much time to spend on each question so that students won't get carried away by less important questions and use their time unwisely.

■ Make it clear whether students are required to stay for the entire time and, if they are, how they may spend any time remaining after they finish.

■ When marking exams, try to be objective. Think about what is on the paper, not who wrote it. Since it is easy after reading an excellent or poor answer to be influenced in judging answers to the next questions on the same paper, I suggest reading and marking the answers to question 1 on all papers, then those for question 2, and so on.

■ Give a separate mark or indication for whatever spelling and punctuation errors do not affect your ability to understand what the writer means. I think it is nonsense to "count off" for spelling when an exam is testing some other subject entirely. Even so, students are probably helped by knowing that you have noticed the mechanics of their papers. If you don't, they get the idea that you only have to spell or punctuate correctly for English classes.

■ Because exams are a wonderful way for students to find out where they went wrong and how they might do better, urge your school to schedule exams in a way that will allow you ample time to discuss them afterwards, both in class and with students who wish to talk to you individually. To miss follow-up wastes the educational potential of an exam.

Preparing for tests and examinations

Following are two sets of suggestions for students: suggestions for reviewing for school tests and exams, and suggestions for taking exams and tests based on school courses. Such suggestions can be made orally or in writing and then be discussed in class. You may duplicate these without further permission.

Reviewing for Tests and Exams

Reviewing intelligently is an excellent way to learn the material of a course. Don't forget, though, that people's styles of learning differ; no one system of studying for tests and examinations works equally well for everyone. The following suggestions may be helpful nevertheless.

1. Assemble all your texts, past tests, and notes you have taken, worksheets given out during the course, and a pencil and paper to make notes as you review.

2. Look over all of the materials you are responsible for mastering. *Don't just reread them.* Remember, you are reviewing, not reading new material for mastery.

   a. Read each heading to see whether you can recall the material that follows. If you can't, read it or skim, if that is enough to recall it to your mind.

   b. Read each underlined or italicized word, each numbered series or list, each item you have marked in any way. Be sure you understand the significance of all these devices.

   c. Look at all exercises and study questions that may be included to be sure that you answer or do all of them. Understand the reason for each.

   d. Memorize any lists, formulas, or rules you are supposed to know.

3. If you have a great deal of material to review and master, make notes on all main points or items. Then review these notes to see whether you recall the material on which they are based. If you recall little or nothing, reread the material.

4. Review carefully all previous tests and be sure you can answer all the questions.

5. If you have questions, write them down and ask them in class a few days before the test, if possible. If some parts seem harder than others, ask the teacher to go over problem areas with you.

6. Try to put yourself in the position of the teacher and think about what kind of test or exam you would give. Make up some practice questions and write or outline answers.

7. Just before the test, reread your notes one last time.

8. Sleep long and well the night before the test so that your mind will be fresh.

Taking Tests and Exams

If you can excel in a test or examination, even though you may not have done as well as you would like in your daily work, you can greatly improve your record. Thinking and writing under pressure, something a test or exam requires, may also be good training for similar challenges in the future. Although test-taking styles differ and people succeed in different ways, the following practices work well for many.

1. Look over the entire test quickly before you start answering any of the questions. Read essay questions right away so that you can be mulling them over even as you work on other parts of the test. Make short notes on various points to avoid losing ideas you have at first reading.

2. Plan your time. Don't spend more time than you should on any one question. Usually the amount of time allotted to a question is related to the amount of credit given for it. Leave a blank space at the end of each answer in case you have time to come back to it and want to write more.

3. Read the directions and questions carefully to avoid the common pitfall of misinterpreting the directions or answering the wrong question because you have misread it.

4. Write legibly but not too slowly. Never waste time copying over an answer on a timed test.

5. If you don't have an answer sheet, be sure you number your answers according to the numbers of the questions. Make it easy for the teacher to follow your paper.

6. Answer first the questions you know best (but don't spend more than the time allotted on them) and do the hardest ones last—unless, of course, you are required to answer the questions in order.

7. Save a few minutes to proofread and revise your answers where needed.

Some comments on test results

When two thirds of a class does poorly on a test or an exam, it is possible that they have been inattentive or that the teaching materials or methods were substandard. In either case, everyone involved — teachers and students — should be shaken a bit. Such a shaking can be healthy, provided it results in better work and better teaching that lead to mastery of the material by almost everyone. Unless a group knows very well that it simply has not done the work, it is bad practice to leave a class with a substantial proportion of no-credit or failing marks among its members. Some reteaching and retesting are probably called for.

There are too many ways of marking tests and exams to discuss them in detail here. Instead, just let me make four more points.

■ Take *great* care in devising a system for marking tests and exams.

■ Explain the system clearly to your classes.

■ Never forget that your marking is at least partly subjective because you are comparing the performance of students with what you think it should be, based on your knowledge of the subject and the skills needed to deal with it on a test.

■ Don't treat your marks with undue reverence, and try to prevent your students from doing so. Marks are somewhat fallible evaluations of a given set of performances at a given time. There is no divine truth in them.

A few more points on testing and evaluation

Before leaving this subject, it is important to make a few more points about what tests are and are not for, how they do and do not work.

■ If a test covers most of the territory dealt with in the course, unit, book, or whatever else is being tested, there is no reason why students should not have it in advance and use it to give direction to their study and review. After all, one of the main purposes of a course is for students to learn the material. If having the test in advance will help them do that, why not? The only exception — an important one — is where the course content to be mastered is much too extensive to be tested on one examination. If students are to be motivated to review and learn all of the material and skills, they should not know in advance just which areas and skills are to be tested on the exam.

■ A similar comment can be made about open-book tests. Unless memorized facts are being tested, using books to answer exam questions can only provide another opportunity to learn. Students should understand, however, that spending most of the test time thumbing through books will not leave them time to write adequate answers.

■ If you have spent a lot of time developing a comprehensive multiple-choice test, or a carefully worked out exam, and if the test or exam works well, keep it and use it another year. For reasons explained just above, it doesn't matter if students see the test in advance. Just be sure that they don't bring a marked answer sheet to the exam.

■ One way to stimulate students to think about what they are learning is to ask them to submit questions for the test or exam in whatever form they prefer, ranging from multiple-choice to essay questions.

■ If you are testing skills, especially reading and dealing with figures, and even spelling and proper use of conventional English, test early enough in the year to leave time to deal with any weaknesses that are discovered. Also, if you discover by test or any other means a remediable academic weakness that has not been dealt with by the end of the school year, or that still needs more work, be sure to pass the word on to the student's next teacher so that special work can be started early the following year.

■ If a student gets low scores in reading or math and you have reason to believe that he or she is intelligent enough to do better, talk to the school's guidance or testing specialist to see about diagnostic testing, which might give more precise evidence on the nature of the problem.

■ It is especially important not to ignore weakness in reading. If some students are reading far below their grade level, the school should support you in efforts to identify and deal with the problem. Because most reading problems are complicated, superficial remedial instruction is usually not enough; scores increase briefly but fall back soon after the special instruction stops. Careful individual or small-group teaching, based on an expert diagnosis of the problem, is necessary. Also, a school should never be satisfied, or try to calm concerned parents, by saying, "Stop worrying; the child will outgrow the problem." Sometimes problems do get outgrown, but more often they don't.

■ The results of standardized tests should be kept in a form that makes them easily available to teachers, without a lot of digging through files. If teachers maintain a professional attitude toward students and their test scores, they can use test information to good advantage, remembering also that scores can give too low or too high an estimate of a student's ability. At the very least, scores tell who is able and should probably be doing better.

■ Some measurement-minded people go hog wild on tests, try to measure everything, and have too little time for things that cannot be measured. Most sensible teachers are satisfied to use measures of what is obviously measurable and continue to teach for the development of the immeasurables. Probably the most important parts of learning—style, expression, appreciation, development of values—cannot be measured by any standardized test.

■ One of the most harmful uses of tests is to rank students in order of ability or in order of scores.

■ Careful observers of young children report that even those who enter the worst schools from the least promising backgrounds enter school expecting to succeed. The idea that they will fail, all too easily converted into the much worse idea that they *are* failures, is something they learn in school. Tests or marks should never be used to teach this terrible thing, "learned helplessness."

19.

Marks and Comments

In the 1960's and 1970's, when much was written against using grades, or marks, a number of forward-looking schools and colleges abandoned grading systems and turned to pass/fail plans. Even at the height of the pass/fail wave, however, only a minute fraction of schools and colleges gave up some sort of traditional marking system. When pass/fail was presented to students as an option rather than a requirement, only a small minority chose it, except in physical education and performance courses, like music and art, in which it is common for schools to make a no-mark evaluation.

Arguments against giving marks

The case against marks, and the research studies that back them up, were convincingly assembled in a lively little book called *Wad-ja-get? The Grading Game in American Education,* by Howard Kirschenbaum, Rodney Napier, and Sidney B. Simon (New York: Hart, 1971). Its arguments, as follows, are not easily dismissed.

■ Marks increase competition and sometimes set one student at war with another.

■ Marks cause cheating. (Many students in high school and college admit to occasional cheating.)

■ Marks are inaccurate measures of performance, mean different things in different schools, to different teachers in the same school and even to the same teacher at different times.

■ Marks provide extraneous motivation and thus stifle love of learning.

■ Marks push teachers into emphasizing gradable content in nicely packaged sets of academic goods that are easily measured and not creative.

■ Marks discourage originality and risk taking on the part of students, encourage parroting, and measure the power of automatic answer giving.

■ Marks spoil teacher-pupil relations by setting teacher against pupil. *Wad-ja-get?* quotes a school consultant on this point: "Each enemy is equipped with vicious weapons. The student has his crib sheets, his ponies, his apple-polishing, rote memorization, fawning obsequiousness, and other kinds of con-artistry. On our side, we teachers resort to mickey-mouse assignments, surprise quizzes, unannounced notebook checks, tricky multiple-choice questions, and irrelevant essay questions."

■ Marks spoil the joy of working.

■ Marks are undemocratic and divisive.

■ Marks are an obstacle to the development of one's self as a person.

■ Marks encourage those who need it least and discourage those who are most in need of encouragement.

■ And, anyway, marks are a relatively recent development, having become common only around the turn of the century, when some sort of easy selection and sorting process was necessary, all the way from professional schools down into the grade schools.

The argument in favor of marks

What's to be said *for* marks? A great deal, and most people in schools and colleges are persuaded by the arguments. Here are some of them.

■ Marks do motivate students to work. Perhaps they shouldn't, but they do, and not all work in school can be made continuously interesting enough to provide steady motivation without them.

■ Marks provide clear, unemotional information. For example, some students do not "hear" an unfavorable comment on a report, but they do hear a D. Many guidance and counseling people insist that children who have no realistic vision of their deficiencies be given regular, even weekly, marks. One boy in a no-mark elementary school was not doing well in his work, so the school psychologist prescribed weekly marks in each "subject." The boy, amazed when he got C's and D's, had been filtering out all the "bad" comments and thought he was an A student.

124

■ Most students want marks so that they may know where they stand (but not on a rank list).

■ Marks provide the quick information about their work that most students need and like.

■ Teachers want to give marks and believe it helps to tell students where they stand.

■ Marks give teachers a convenient, workable system of record keeping that lets them know where individual students stand, how they are progressing, and what they need in the way of special work and help.

■ Marks stimulate students to ask "How can I do better?" and, in the upper grades, "What are the goals of this course, and how do you measure me against them?"—good, motivating questions.

■ Finally, marks provide a commonly understood means of transfer from school to school, to college, to professional school, and even sometimes to the world of work.

If marks, starting when?

No sensible person would advocate a system of marks in kindergarten or first grade. When do we start marking? In the early grades, schools should strive to keep children "awash with encouragement." What they do needs immediate evaluation, but in forms less abstract than a mark.

Fifth grade, or possibly fourth, is about the right time to begin marks and comments. By age nine or ten, most girls and boys tend to feel as secure about themselves as they ever will; most of them can read, write, and figure; they like life, school, and teachers; and they like acquiring information and skills. Realistic and ready for realism, they are ready to be introduced to the full marking system of the school they are in, whatever it may be. It is not necessary to ease them gradually into the idea of marks. A clear explanation of what marks are and why schools use them, accompanied by a concise written version of the marking system and an opportunity to discuss marks as a way of giving information about a student's work, are all that is needed. Furthermore, it is easier for students at the secure age of ten to adjust to a system of marks than it would be later, in their early teens, when they are dealing with the turmoil of adolescence.

What system works best?

The two chief characteristics of a sound marking system are that it does not make unrealistically fine distinctions and that its terms or symbols are clearly defined or explained. Regardless of one's own convictions or preferences, the best policy is to understand fully and adopt the system your school uses, to be sure your students understand it, and to stress to them that the only purpose of marks is to convey information that will help them to further learning.

A marking system that works well for a good many schools is A and A− = excellent, B+ = very good, B = good, B− = fairly good, C+ and C = fair, C− = barely fair, D = poor, and NC = no credit. (Note that C does not mean "average.") Whatever system is used, try to avoid using the common mark F for "failing." It is a heavy term and may connote failure as a person in addition to denoting failure of work. If your school does use F−a strong message that many teachers feel is educational−take special care to see that your students know it refers to their work, not to themselves.

What marks mean

One great trouble with marks, especially those given to students to evaluate their work on a long paper, a unit, or a whole year's work, is that so many different judgments get summed up and set down in a single symbol. What does "C" mean? If the course was characterized by continuing communication between teacher and student, the meaning of C may be clear to the student. Will it be clear to the student's parents? Almost certainly not, beyond the definition published−in the case of C, "fair." But what kind of "fair"?

"Fair" might mean the performance of a student who is dutiful and careful and whose work is mechanically correct but lacks originality and depends largely on the teacher's organization and presentations. Or a student whose work is marred by serious mechanical errors but who demonstrates fairly good comprehension of the main ideas of the course.

Therefore, if enlightening communication about papers, projects, units, and courses is to take place, marks must be accompanied by comments. Here are the kinds of comments that illuminate the marks on a report card.

B   Julius spells well but punctuates carelessly. The content of his written work is excellent. Julius should read more and better books. He is an excellent discusser when he pays attention, but too often the teacher has to call for his attention.

D   Despite the D, Josie's situation is not hopeless. Her last two papers were fair, and she seems to be learning from her extra sessions. She must learn to be more careful about mechanics.

C   Jack has an able mind that he is not using to capacity. He does well on tests, but his computation is careless and his assignments often are late and poorly done.

D   This is a hard subject for Jim. His memory for sounds is underdeveloped, and he seems discouraged. Often he is not attentive. We are giving him extra help. It is time for a conference.

A   Jessica's project on worms was excellently done. She is creative in her daily work, and our main challenge is to keep her interested.

None of these comments judges the student as a person. All focus on performance, are factual, and, where needed, make a suggestion for improvement or indicate that help is being provided.

In the following sample comments on papers, no marks are shown, though these papers would be marked—a mark for content, a mark for spelling, and a mark for mechanics.

This held my interest, and the ending made me laugh. The stars show three places that should have been more fully developed.

Read your papers *aloud* to catch run-on sentences.

Good beginning, confusing ending; rewrite last page. How much time did you spend on this? Please see me.

You don't seem to have spent enough effort on this to make it worth marking. Please redo.

Very well put together, but the evidence is very slight. Give more examples to support statements.

You report facts clearly, but what are your conclusions? What did you set out to show? Be clear about your purpose before you start.

Some further suggestions

Here are some further suggestions about marks and comments.

■ To see how fallible you are, try grading a set of papers twice, not writing on them the first time but recording your marks in a separate place. If you can do so—though usually you shouldn't keep papers this long—let a week or ten days go by between markings. You may be surprised how your two ratings of the same papers differ.

■ To save time on comments, if you have many students, a heavy schedule, and little time to write comments, give separate marks for effort (making it clear that this is only your impression), for classroom conduct, for promptness in turning in work, and even, if sloppiness is a widespread problem, for neatness of work. But never try to average these marks into a single mark. There is no unridiculous way to average the properties, appearance, and behavior of elephants, fleas, violets, and jellyfish.

■ Mark students only on their performance, never on their ability. Some teachers give students good marks just because they are bright. Others give low marks for the same reason if the performance is only good but not as good as they think it should be. A mark should be based on a standard of performance. Students have a right to know where their performance stands in relation to an external standard of measurement.

■ Be cautious about giving an unrealistically high mark because you think a student needs encouragement. This practice is likely to backfire next time.

■ For very special work a student may be required to do and for which you really don't want to give a conventional mark yet need some kind of indication in your record book, since you consider the task an important part of the total work—a freely written daily journal, for example—devise a special, neutral set of symbols, such as RS = really something, S = something, NM = not much, as far as I can tell, and N = nothing, as far as I can tell. Be sure to explain to the class what these mean and write them and their meanings down where students may refer to them. With such marks, you will have some kind of record in your book when the time comes to evaluate students' total performance at the end of a grading period.

128

■ If the question "Wad-ja-get?" circulates feverishly around the classroom when papers, tests, or reports are handed back, be ready to say, "That's the wrong question. Ask yourself what marks and comments tell *you* about *your* work. Remember, marks are information. Use them that way. Any questions?"

20.

Reports to Students and Parents

Obviously, at least in the upper grades, marks and comments are closely linked to reports. Probably your school has an established form for making reports to students and their parents. Be sure you understand how it works and how you are supposed to use it. Also, be sure that your students and their families understand it.

Reports sent home in middle and upper grades

If marks are given, a good report form will include the definition of each mark. If it doesn't, a slip giving definitions should be enclosed with the report so that all concerned will understand what each symbol means.

When you write comments on a report sent home, it is wise to stick to facts. It is also pointless to say, "Very good work," when a B+ already says that. Perhaps "Nice going, John," will make John feel good, but it is even better to tell him what is so good. Worse is "You can do better, John," or "You should do better," without any clue to how he should do better. Most competent reports say something encouraging and add a suggestion or two about how the student might improve.

The customary purpose of a report is to give an account of the status and progress of the student in your subject. It should enlighten the student and the parents about the student's strengths and weaknesses in the subject and, perhaps, as a member of the class. It should suggest how the student might do better. If the subject is one involving basic skills (reading, writing, computation, logical thinking, organization), at some time early in the year you should report on the state of these skills inso-far as you have evidence about them. Be sure to look at last year's reports first to make sure you are not reporting, without recognizing and explaining it, something quite different from what last year's teacher said. You may also want to say something about how these skills show themselves in class and schoolwork as compared to the measures on standardized tests, but it is best, as I have said, not to give actual test scores.

You should avoid certain pitfalls when writing reports, as follows.

■ Don't play psychiatrist. Leave deep analysis of the student's charac-ter or family and other relationships to counselors and specialists. If some-thing concerns personal or family adjustment, it is better to talk about it in a conference than in writing. In a written report, stick to observed facts from which the parents and the student can draw conclusions, per-haps with your help. Stick to what you know.

■ Avoid cleverness and even humor. Reports are usually taken very seriously by those who read them. If you sound light and witty rather than straightforward, you run a danger. Especially avoid sarcasm. I remem-ber once writing about an amiable, popular, lazy sixth grader, "Paul is filled with love, but love is not enough." This was true, but Paul's mother still quotes it to me as a piece of irreverence—and irrelevance—that they did not appreciate.

■ Don't predict. By saying "I am sure Sally will do much better dur-ing the next marking period," you may mean to encourage Sally, but if she doesn't do better, you are left in an awkward position. Why hasn't she done better? Probably because you haven't taught her properly. It is better to say, "Sally can do better, I think, and here are a few suggestions . . ."

■ If in doubt when writing the first report of the year, mark on the low side but make your comments as encouraging and constructive as possi-ble. It is much better to be able to report improvement as the year goes on than to have to back away from an unsound judgment made earlier. Some students do go downhill during the year for reasons that may be entirely beyond your control, so if Polly is having a midwinter slump, report that fact to her parents and to her.

■ Don't write comments that make you sound ineffectual—"I just don't know what to do about Billy's talking in class," "How can we teach Mary not to hand in so many late papers?" Their parents will probably just say, out of frustration, "Well, what are we supposed to do about it? That's your job." It is better to say, "Billy has to learn to control himself in class so that the teacher doesn't have to. I have made some suggestions to him," or "For the past two weeks I have been keeping Mary after school when she handed her papers in late. I hope she will soon learn to meet deadlines."

■ Don't put off pointing out a weakness or a problem that may cause trouble later in the year, like inability to do simple arithmetic, a very slow reading rate, or inability to concentrate for more than a few minutes. Parents want and students need to know about such fundamental problems early so that they and the school can tackle them as soon as possible. Many a parent has been justifiably disaffected, and many a child put at a disadvantage, by teachers' unfounded hopes that problems will simply be outgrown without attention or help. Often they are, and then everyone is happy; if they aren't, time is wasted. A low-key early-warning policy is valuable.

■ If reports are handed out to students as a group, don't allow a frantic, whispered round of "Wad-ja-get?" Too many students feel hurt, embarrassed, and helpless in such a situation. Instead, be sure to tell students they have the right to keep their reports to themselves and that reports are meant for giving information, not for comparing. Take enough time to discuss this so that students really understand and accept it, and then enforce the no-comparing rule while they are in your room.

■ Even though reports are addressed to parents and are to be taken home and shown to Mom and Dad, probably their most important function is what they say to the student: "Alan, your work since January . . ." No matter to whom addressed, the message should be one that will help the student, who should not be talked about as if he or she were an absent, nonreading nonentity.

■ Sometimes it is useful to hand out reports to students at a time when they can discuss them individually with you while the rest of the class work independently at their desks. In this way, any obvious misunderstandings can be cleared up before the reports go home. It is best to let students read their reports first and then to ask those who wish to do so to talk with you briefly. If it is clear that a long conference is needed, schedule it for later to let others who need to have at least a moment to raise their quick questions. If you are quite sure that some students are too shy to ask to see you, take the initiative by asking them if they want to see you.

■ If one isn't provided, make a copy of what you have written about each student for reference or later conference purposes.

■ Don't make the mistake of thinking that the mark on a final report for the year must be some sort of average of the marks and reports for all the grading periods or units during the year. In cumulative subjects like mathematics and languages, but also to a considerable degree in English, history, and science, the most important question to consider at the end of the year is "How competent is this student to do work in this subject now, after all the ups and downs of the year?" The important thing is for students to learn to *do* history or science or English, not to memorize them or store them up in unit-sized, labeled morsels.

■ Encourage parents to respond to their children's reports. By being able to reply in writing or in a conference, they can give you insights that may help you teach their children better.

■ It is not a bad idea to encourage, but not require, students to write responses to their reports. It stimulates them to think about what their reports said, and it may give you helpful reactions. Some teachers ask students to write their own reports and give themselves marks before the teacher writes the students' reports. This is another way to get students to think about their attitudes, performance, and aptitudes.

Reports about younger children

Much about reports for the middle and upper grades also applies to the lower grades and kindergarten. Since it is unlikely that marks will be given until fourth or fifth grade, many schools and teachers prefer, at least during the first half of the school year, to have conferences instead of sending a written report home. One danger of not making a written report, though, is that parents will not "hear" what you are telling them about their children, and no record of it will exist in case problems come up later and parents complain, "Nobody ever told us." Perhaps it is best, therefore, to have a written report accompany your oral report to parents.

In a conference, it helps to have a checklist to make sure that nothing really important is overlooked. On the other hand, you don't have to go over every item on the list because it is there; just concentrate on the particular points that apply to the student being discussed.

Here is a sample checklist. You can fill in the details as they fit your school's situation. By keeping the list informal, you will help to put parents at ease and in the mood to talk. You and the parents should each have a copy to refer to as you talk.

Checklist for Parent-Teacher Conferences

1. Any outstanding problems or concerns of parents, teachers, child?

2. How about the child's basic skills and attitudes toward them — in reading, writing, math (arithmetic), speaking, discussing, study skills?

3. How about other schoolwork, homework, motivation in general?

4. Any home problems that interfere with school, or vice versa?

5. How about recreation and free time?

6. How about health and physical considerations?

7. Social adjustment?

8. Personality?

9. Any problems we agreed on? Follow-up action? Anything special to talk with the child about? If so, who to do the talking? Should we meet again?

Here are two last, very important points about parent conferences.

■ Do your best to be honest, to stick to what you know, and not to make things look better or worse than they are for the student or for the school.

■ Never blame parents. Parents almost always try as hard as they can, perhaps against odds and forces you know nothing about, and they don't need blaming. And never let your words or voice take on a scolding tone.

Parent-teacher conferences at any level

Parent-teacher conferences are a form of reporting. I have been in many such conferences, often as a parent, more often as a teacher, where time was wasted or poorly used. Here are some ideas, in addition to the checklist, for overcoming that problem.

■ Remember that students are one person but that their lives are divided into at least two parts: home and school. If you and the parents can work together, the student is likely to benefit. Therefore, if possible, at least through eighth grade, teachers should try to talk with the parents of each student at least once a year to see how things are going.

■ Unless parent-teacher conferences are routinely scheduled, ask parents to call school for an appointment. If parents happen to run into you and want to talk right then, feel perfectly free to say you're busy just then and ask whether they can talk to you later at a specified time.

■ When parents want to see you, encourage them to tell you ahead of time what they especially want to talk about so that you can prepare for the conversation. You may want to check with other teachers.

■ Plunge right into the subject of the conference. It is tempting to ease into things by talking about the weather or politics or the recent school play instead of spending time on what the parents really want to talk about. Make a point of saying, almost right away, "Well, let's see; we're going to talk about Bob's difficulty in math," or "Do you want to start with your questions about Julie, or shall I tell you a couple of things we have on our minds?"

■ Remember that most school problems are rather complicated, and that simple answers are not likely to be useful. Therefore, be cautious when a parent says, "I only need five minutes of your time." It is almost certain to take longer; if you don't allow more time, both you and the parents will leave unsatisfied. Once a mother saw me in the hall, asked for "just five minutes," sat down with a sigh, and said, "We are convinced our daughter can't spell and doesn't understand what she's reading. What should we do?"

■ Often it can be more helpful to include the student in the conference than to talk about him or her in absentia. I realize that this is a rather revolutionary idea, but when students aren't present, it means that parents or teachers must explain later what went on, perhaps not as accurately or as impressively as letting the student hear it all in the first place. If students are present, they can't play teacher and parent off against each other. Also, many students feel that it isn't quite fair for adults—even loving, intelligent ones—to talk about them when they aren't there. They may not need or want to defend themselves, but often right in the conference they can explain and express feelings. If the student is to be there, parents and teachers must not act or seem to act as a powerful double hammer of authority. The student needs a chance to talk and explain and react. It is obviously more appropriate for a ninth grader to be at a conference than for a fourth grader. And some feelings (anger, deep discouragement, distrust) and topics (the methods a teacher uses, fundamental objections to the school, suspected need for psychiatric evaluation or treatment) are better discussed, at least in the early stages, without the student present.

■ If definite action is agreed upon in a conference, it helps to confirm the agreement in a brief note, with a copy for the student's folder.

■ If possible, begin and end the conference on a positive, but true, note.

Grade meetings of parents

An excellent and efficient way to get in touch with parents and keep them informed about their children's lives in school, about school, and about what and how you are teaching is to call a meeting of all the parents of your class as early in the year as you have learned the names of most of your students and a little about them, which probably means the middle of October. Such meetings, whose tone should be kept informal but not casual, can be presided over by the principal, division head, grade head, or a teacher who is good at this kind of thing. In preparing your presentation, which you give when parents break up into groups with their child's teacher, you might consider the following ideas.

■ Explain clearly and specifically what you hope to teach the students this year and how you expect to go about it.

■ Tell parents how they can help. If the best help is for them to do nothing, so that you can know how well students are working and thinking entirely on their own, say so.

■ Unless the school discourages it, or unless it makes you uncomfortable, invite parents to visit your class whenever they wish to. Usually they won't, but they like to feel they can, and when they do it is almost always beneficial.

■ Be careful not to claim that "this grade" is "*the* crucial, watershed year" of a student's education. This may be true, but it probably isn't, and when parents hear teacher after teacher say it year after year, they get skeptical. Just tell them why what you are doing with students is important and what you hope their children will accomplish.

■ Say whether you are or are not willing to be called at home and under what, if any, circumstances. Some teachers enjoy telephone conferences, which can be extremely useful.

■ Encourage parents to write a note early in the year to the homeroom teacher or some other person who is in touch with their child's teachers if they have any points they particularly want not to be forgotten – "Please be sure to seat Barry near the front of the room so that he will pay attention, because he won't sit there unless you ask him to," or "Maud had math tutoring all summer. If she seems to need more, we'd like to know right away. It got her through quite well last year."

21.
Keeping in Touch

One of my favorite stories about not being enough in touch with the feelings of other people is that of the eight-year-old girl and her small brother who were on the loose in the Neiman-Marcus department store in Dallas one hot afternoon. The children had bought ice cream cones and were amusing themselves by riding the escalators. They were jammed together with other passengers, and the boy, noticing that his cone was dripping, wiped it on the mink stole of the woman in front of him. His sister cried out, "Watch out, Johnny! You're getting fur all over your ice cream."

This epitomizes the human condition; we have great difficulty in seeing things from any point of view but our own. Teachers should, by example, precept, and planned experiences, get their students to try to put themselves in the situation of others, to see things from others' points of view, and, further, to explain to others their own point of view, situation, and feelings. We should constantly be teaching the art and science of keeping in touch with one another.

Teaching should not be just a one-way flow of information and directions from the full, dynamic teacher into the empty, docile student, but an exchange—sometimes quiet, sometimes lively—of ideas, questions, and points of view. A good school, or even a good classroom in an otherwise stiff and noncommunicating school, offers lots of vital exchange and many opportunities for the wearers of stoles and the eaters of ice cream to know one another.

Keeping in touch with students

John Holt, in *How Children Fail* (New York: Pitman, 1964), writes, "A teacher in a class is like a man in the woods at night with a powerful flashlight in his hand. Wherever he turns his light, the creatures on whom it shines are aware of it, and do not behave as they do in the dark. Thus the mere fact of his watching their behavior changes it into something very different. Shine where he will, he can never know very much of the night life of the woods." If our "watching" is like an intimidating beam of light in an otherwise dark room filled with frightened creatures, we had better look for some more general sources of light for all.

One source can be our own willingness to let our students see us as human beings with problems, frailties, and feelings, just like other people, and not simply as The Teacher. Some openness on our part may beget openness on the part of our students. This doesn't mean "inflicting personal opinions on the class," or "crying in class," to mention two traits students say they object to.

What it means is admitting when we are wrong, showing that we feel great or terrible on this day or that, revealing that we can be hurt or made to feel good by what our students say and do, and that we, too, miss deadlines, can't get down to work sometimes, lose things, and often would rather play than work. We can exemplify—or at least not try too hard to hide—our humanity without becoming unprofessional. Simply saying, on occasion, "Let me tell you how that makes me feel" helps keep them in touch with us and opens them to putting us in touch with them.

The other side of it, of course, is for us to keep ourselves as informed and aware as we can be of the state of mind and emotions of our students as well as of their academic progress or lack of it. Here are some suggestions for keeping in touch.

■ Some of us grind on through our lesson plans, our schemes, and our subjects, intent on *our* purposes and goals, until we have allowed ourselves to get out of touch with the lives and learning of our students. It is therefore a good idea to stop and ask, from time to time, "How are things going?" or "Is anything bothering anybody?" and then listen to the answers.

■ Sometimes it is better to hand out a sheet for students to fill out anonymously if they wish, reporting their concerns and reactions. It can be as simple as "How are things going? (1) With you and this class? (2) With my teaching? (3) Any suggestions for me? (4) Anything I should know about you? about others?"

■ Deal with group problems in class meetings and with individual problems by talking with students. At times, though, it is good just to help students get their feelings out into the open. Sometimes adults unconsciously underrate the feelings of children and students, starting at a very early age: "It doesn't hurt that much" (when it hurts a lot), "You don't really mind missing the party" (when you really feel terrible about missing it), "Why, we all *love* the baby and are *glad* we have him" (when you really wish you could make him disappear). We should not tell students they don't feel what they know they feel, because that doesn't change feelings or eliminate them; it just drives them underground, where they may do a lot of harm. Accepting and understanding a person's feelings is one way of keeping communications open. When someone is being difficult or unpleasant, it doesn't help to cheer them, forbid them, condemn them, or reason with them, because such actions ignore the feelings. Help get the feelings out, then try the reasoning.

■ We should accept our students' feelings, but we don't have to accept all their actions. You can try to make it clear that people are not responsible for their feelings, but that they are, or should be, responsible for their actions. Students need to learn that sometimes expressing a feeling is an action: "Jake, I really hate you!" Jake's classmate, at least for the moment, probably does feel hate, but he must learn not to hurt others by the act of expressing hostility in a damaging way.

■ Try to make yourself available for students to talk to, even though in most schools there simply isn't time, unless you open your class periods to allow it. But it is not only a question of being available; it is also a question of students being able to talk to you. When I asked 400 students in grades 5-9 "Is it difficult for you to talk satisfactorily with your teachers about questions important to you?" 22 per cent said "Yes," 44 per cent said "At times," and 34 per cent said "No." Then I asked, "If it is difficult, why?" Some of their answers are instructive. Fifth and sixth graders said, "She doesn't have time, the room is not very private, and she often doesn't understand a word I say," "They're too busy," "I'm shy," "I'm afraid," "They're not my father or mother." Students in grades 7-9 said, "They don't care," "They'd get mad and yell," "They don't really listen," "They're always right," "I've never considered talking to a teacher about anything," "I wouldn't want them to know about me." So our job is not easy.

■ Before and after classes, during recess, in the morning and afternoon, as you work at your desk, listen to the student chitchat — not eavesdropping, just taking in the scene. You may learn a lot that will help you keep in touch.

■ A good way to learn indirectly how students are feeling and what they are thinking is to use the technique of role playing. It not only helps you to keep in touch with them but helps them to communicate with one another and with others outside. For example, after a fight over a serious difference of opinion has cooled down, ask the antagonists to try to take each other's point of view and defend it in an argument. If it's too heated for them to do so, ask two other students to pay the roles of the antagonists and then let the class discuss the actions and words. Occasionally, you can take part in role playing, too — being one of the student antagonists, or asking a student to play you and you playing a type of student who annoys you — and then talk about it. Role playing is usually a fairly painless, and often very funny, way of bringing out truths and forces that would be too painful to talk about directly.

■ If you can get a visiting day, spend it in your own school following the program — *all day* — of students in a class you teach. It is amazing what a variety of circumstances, personalities, standards of discipline, and expectations that students adjust to with seeming success. In a way, they are like water poured into vessels of different shapes; they take on the shape of each vessel, rarely spilling or boiling over.

■ Keep in touch with students by maintaining good records in your own record book so that you can remind yourself at a glance where each student is, at least in some important respects.

■ Since television is such an important influence on the lives of students, and often, whether you like it or not, their minds and feelings are much more impressed by television programs than anything else, make yourself watch some of the programs they watch. If you are book-oriented, this can be hard to do, but try it so that you will at least understand students' television allusions in class and be able, to a degree, to empathize with their viewing. If you don't know where to begin, ask students for suggestions or pick up ideas from conversations you hear.

Keeping in touch with colleagues

In some schools, some teachers pour all their being into their own classroom-castles, to which they repair at start of day and from which they flee at the end, meeting colleagues only at faculty meetings, in the hall, and, if necessary, at lunch.

In other schools, teachers are the center of one another's social lives. They meet, eat, gossip, picnic, study, and party together, sometimes joyfully, sometimes with the grim purpose of knowing one another in every dimension and thus of improving. It is fine for teachers to be friends and socialize if they enjoy it and it happens easily, but most of us will be better teachers if we reserve a good portion of our lives for the normal world outside of school and try to keep in touch with the main currents of life.

Even so, within the school day and on the school premises, there are many ways we can and should keep in touch with one another for our own sakes and for the sakes of our students.

■ Do talk shop. What could be more interesting, if you like your work, than talking about it? I have never understood why people feel they have to say, "Excuse me for talking shop, but . . ."

■ Use the lunch table, or an unplanned five minutes in the hall, as a ready-made, effortless occasion for sharing ideas and working out the hundreds of little coordinations and passings of information that make schools work well—"doing business on the hoof." It's even all right to compare notes on individual students, provided they are somewhere else and provided you aren't just gossiping.

■ The faculty room is an even better place than lunch to let your hair down and express your pleasures, worries, and frustrations. If your school has no faculty room, it should.

■ Visit your colleagues' classes and invite them to visit yours. It helps if a school's staff members can be open enough with one another to enter and leave classrooms without having it be an event. A few five- or ten-minute glimpses often provide more healthy material for communication than an entire forty-five-minute period planned in advance and sat through dutifully. After visits, you can compare notes and give and receive ideas, approaches, and methods for working with students and subjects that weeks of faculty meetings cannot provide.

■ Use free periods you have in common with other teachers to plan and talk. Never assume, though, that just because a teacher is sitting alone in an empty room he or she is available. Ask first, before plunging in.

■ Try to schedule an occasional meeting, or even regular meetings, of all the teachers of a given grade to compare notes and to discuss especially difficult students, students who need more challenge, or those who never seem to attract attention.

■ Occasionally, cut across dividing lines by holding interdepartmental meetings, meetings of department heads, or meetings of teachers of several consecutive grades. Sometimes we forget what important work other people are doing.

■ Never encourage, even with the best of motives, a whole class to talk with you or in your presence about their objections to and difficulties with another teacher. You may want to listen just long enough to get the gist of the problem, in case you can think of a way to help the teacher, but almost always the best policy is to tell your students, "Talk it over with Mr. X. After all, you and he are the ones who need to work it out." If you know Mr. X well enough, you can, with due caution and hesitation, tell him what seems to be coming up and what you said to your class.

■ The opposite side of students' objections and difficulties is the good work we and our colleagues do. If you hear students expressing their enthusiasm for a teacher's class or for a project, or if you pass by a classroom and see a lively class in progress and stop in for a minute and are impressed by what is going on, make a point of telling the teacher the good things you have seen and heard. We all thrive on honest, well-founded praise and recognition.

■ And, finally, faculty meetings – the best places to communicate and the worst. They are best when faculty and administration plan the agenda together; when substantive issues – teaching, curriculum, testing – come first and little announcements last, when people are too weary to quibble over them; when everyone feels free to speak out; and when the goal is not to win points or to prevail but to reach a consensus by which all can work constructively. Faculty meetings are at their worst when they turn into gripe sessions, when they are devoted to scolding or to pep talks, and when most people can't wait to get out of the meeting to say what they really think. Make it a rule to say it in the meeting, if it's important, or not to say it at all – at least for twenty-four hours, and then to say it to someone who can help solve rather than aggravate the problem.

Keeping in touch with "the administration"

John Coleman, former president of Haverford College, said, "In actuality, a president is at the center of a web of conflicting interest groups, none of which can ever be fully satisfied. He is, by definition, almost always wrong. . . . It's all very interesting, and not hard to take once he gets over wanting to be right and settles instead for doing the best he can." Coleman could just as well have been talking about school heads, most of whom find it a mighty challenge to reach the state of maturity he describes.

One important way to keep in touch with "the administration" is to try to understand what their lives are like. School heads and principals often are perceived by teachers and students as being relatively rich; protected from the daily grind and pressures by a competent secretary; inhabiting a spacious, well-furnished office on the quiet side of the school; consorting with the movers and shakers, usually at lunch off the premises; keeping for themselves those things they like to do and delegating everything else; enjoying the exercise of power; and not having any papers to mark in the evenings.

Consider the following facts about the lives of principals.

They don't have the luxury of shooting off their mouths because what they say is heard as The Institution Speaking. They aren't allowed to complain; it's too catching.

144

They get to know hundreds of people slightly and few people intimately. Everybody knows them, but they can't know everybody, even though they are expected to.

They rarely get easy problems to solve. Only the toughest ones reach their desks. They have to make hundreds of small decisions quickly, and often with inadequate evidence, for sometimes making no decision is worse than making an imperfect decision.

They have to hear all sides and suspend judgment while advocates, complainers, and demands for action (or for stopping action) press upon them. Their brains and desks are a tangle (or an ordered web) of suspended judgments. They have to conduct an orchestra of cacophonous interests and concerns and often compose the score while conducting. They must hear cacophony but broadcast harmony. Some of the harmony should be well-presented challenges and questions to the school.

Most of their problems never go away; they just have to be dealt with in new forms. Thus heads risk feeling like the frustrated Australian who got a new boomerang and spent the rest of his life trying to throw the old one away.

They have to give credit to others for all the good things that happen and take or expect no credit for themselves. Conversely, if something goes wrong, from furnace to advanced calculus, it's their fault—or someone thinks it is.

They have to be ready to say something on all public occasions, thus running the deadly professional hazard of not recognizing that they don't have anything to say.

They can never say their work is done.

For a really good school head or principal, the main reward is probably the inner satisfaction that comes from giving one's all and feeling that, on the whole, the job is well done. But heads are human, and occasionally they need praise and encouragement.

They need to be told they've done a good job when they have—"That speech was right to the point," "The new science teacher told me what a great help your visit was and how many good ideas she got from it."

They need to be shown that their colleagues recognize that their life is tough—"I don't see how you manage to keep so much in mind the way you do," "I know you had a meeting this morning and have a meeting to-night, so I'll be quick."

They need now and then to hear someone in a faculty or parents' meeting report the facts about a problem and then suggest a solution based on the needs of the entire school, now and future, with good humor and caring, without any ego involved.

And they need to have someone available, either in school or outside, with whom they can be utterly honest, unpremeditated, tentative, troubled, distressed, or exultant, knowing that what is said will be passed on to no one — but no one.

I have two other suggestions for keeping in touch with the administration.

Do not assume that, just because their doors are closed, administrators are not willing to see you. If you have a concern you wish to share, make an appointment, preferably for a day or two hence so that you can be sure it's worth talking about. Don't storm the door in anger and go away feeling rejected. When making your appointment, write a short note explaining what you want to talk about so that the administrator can prepare for your conference.

Invite administrators to visit your classes. The best administrators will appreciate this, and good administrators are also competent at "doing business on the hoof," identifying problems, becoming aware of feelings, and seeing and remembering always that most of the business of the school is in classrooms, including yours, with a considerable overflow into the halls between periods.

The ablest school principal I know once neatly defined his unneat job: "I must be the resident futurist and diagnostician." By this he meant that the job of heads is to keep the entire school in their minds and to know where it has come from and where it should be going, and at the same time to be alert to where the serious trouble spots are that might develop into widespread problems, and to give those trouble spots effective treatment.

Trustees and school boards

Too many of us cut ourselves off psychologically from the boards that govern our schools or school systems by assuming that they could some-

146

how, if they really wanted to, establish the policies and especially provide the money to solve the problems of the school we are in. It is a careless sort of luxury to blame board members for school problems and inadequacies, of which they are probably very much aware and with which they are trying to grapple.

One of the most unwise actions a teacher can take, unless members of the faculty are expressly invited to do so, is to get into private conversation with a board member about a specific operational matter. If you feel there is something that the board really needs to know and does not know, speak about it first with the head of the school or someone else on the staff who meets with the board. After that, if you still feel that the board needs to hear from you, ask the head how best to go about being heard.

The other side of the coin is that board members should never get involved in the daily operations of the school, beyond making a suggestion on a take-it-or-leave-it basis. The line between determination of policy and daily operation of schools should be clearly drawn.

Board members should be encouraged to visit the school, to observe classes, and to talk with students and teachers about what is going on in the school so that they will gain the background they need when called upon to develop and determine policy. You as a teacher can help in this by encouraging those you know to come and see.

Keeping in touch with the world

It is easy to become so immersed in school that we lose touch with the world outside. We tend to see everything from our view at the center of the world, the center being the classroom or our subject. I have some suggestions.

■ From time to time, no matter how many papers you have to deal with or projects to prepare, put them aside, count on a couple of days of easy lessons or reading and consultation periods, and relax for a weekend, enjoy yourself, and don't think about school. Be in touch with whatever world there is outside of school. Another idea is to mark, *in ink,* on your calendar, *well in advance,* some afternoons and evenings, or weekends, when you plan a school-empty time. Then, if someone from school mentions that time, you can say, looking at your calendar, "I'm sorry, I'm busy then."

■ Another part of the world outside our schools and classrooms is our broader professional world. If we are to be in touch with this part of reality, we should do professional reading. Colleagues and the school's librarian are the best initial sources of information about books, journals, and other reading. As you read more, you will discover other leads to follow on your own. Talking about reading with other teachers is one of the best ways of all of keeping in touch.

22.

Getting Your Own Teaching Evaluated

A major complaint of new and experienced teachers alike is that they really don't know how well they are doing their jobs and that nobody is willing to tell them. On the other hand, teachers almost universally object to being officially evaluated by their schools, especially if that evaluation is tied to any kind of merit rating that will affect their salaries, and especially if the evaluation is based on a long, complex form filled out by a supervisor during or just after a single class period visit.

Since this book is mainly for teachers, not administrators, I shall stay away from the sticky question of merit ratings and instead concentrate on how you, a teacher, can get your work evaluated if you really care to do so—and you should.

Teacher-made evaluation

One of the best ways to have your teaching evaluated, by yourself or by anyone else, including students, is to make a list of questions about your work and ask people to reply to them. You will find parts of the following set of questions useful, though you will probably need to adapt other parts to your own situation. Clearly, some of the questions are better suited to teachers of grade 7 and up than to those of elementary grades.

Evaluation of the teaching of   (name)

Please rate this teacher from 1 to 5, with 1 = Always, 2 = Usually, 3 = Sometimes, 4 = Seldom, 5 = Never. Feel free to add comments.

    1. Does the teacher have a good knowledge of the subject? ____

2. Is the teacher enthusiastic about the subject? ____
3. Are the goals of the course clear? ____
4. Is the teacher organized and well prepared for class? ____
5. Does the teacher explain the material clearly? ____
6. Is class time flexible enough to allow for unplanned questions that come up? ____
7. Is the teacher on time for classes? ____
8. Is the teacher able to maintain a reasonable level of order and an atmosphere that encourages learning? ____
9. Are deadlines enforced fairly? ____
10. Is the workload (tests, papers, homework) distributed fairly evenly throughout the marking period? ____
11. Are tests and papers returned to the student within a reasonable amount of time? ____
12. Are tests and papers marked and commented on helpfully? ____
13. Does the teacher respect the students? ____
14. Is the teacher available when students need help? ____
15. Does the teacher show an interest in students' progress and success in the course? ____
16. Does the homework help students learn the subject? ____
17. Is the teacher respected? ____
18. Do the students respect one another? ____
19. Do the students cut class? ____
20. Are the students on time to class? ____
21. Do the students come to class prepared? ____
22. Do the students participate in class? ____
23. Does the teacher treat the students fairly? ____
24. The tests in this course are (circle one):
       Too hard   Challenging but fair   Adequate   Too easy
25. The teacher's grading practices are (circle one):
       Fair   Unclear   Unfair
26. The rate of covering material is (circle one):
       Too fast   Satisfactory   Too slow
27. List any strong points about the course and the teacher you would like to mention:
28. List any course material you feel should be modified or replaced:
29. List any weak points about the course and the teacher and suggestions for improvement:
30. Please feel free to add any other comments you wish to make.

150

How do you use the answers to a questionnaire like this?

■ No matter how good you are, or think you are, be prepared for some shocks. If students answer honestly, some will see flaws and suggest improvements. Some suggestions will be genuine and helpful, and some will be impossible or born out of a student's own problems and resentments, which may arise from conditions having nothing to do with you or your teaching. I have seen some teachers—fine ones—be so shaken and discouraged by the frank opinions of a few of their students that they became less confident, able teachers as a result.

■ If you want honest answers, permit students not to sign their names. However, if they do sign their names you will know whom to seek out if you have things you want to ask questions about. Explain also that what students say on their evaluation sheet will have no effect on how you judge their work. This might be a suitable time to explain that, with exceptions such as this, anonymous notes and letters are not a good idea and that people should be willing to stand by their opinions.

■ Give the questionnaire to other people—colleagues, administrators, supervisors, assistant teachers—whose opinions you value and ask them to answer those questions on which they have an opinion.

■ One trouble with most evaluations of teachers is that they are done at the end of a course or the end of the year, when nobody can benefit but the teacher and the teacher's new students the following year. I therefore suggest that you use the questionnaire during the school year, not just at the end. Students are most interested in evaluating teaching when they know that something can be done about opinions they express. So as soon as you feel that your students are acquainted with the methods, manner, and content of your teaching, tell them that you would be helped by a frank evaluation and that you really want their opinions (if they want to give them) to help you plan for the rest of the year. Somewhere around Thanksgiving is the right time, with possibly another, shorter evaluation in February, and then a final one at the end of the year. The one most valuable for you and your students is the Thanksgiving evaluation, since it gives you plenty of time to use the results.

■ Try to find a time to discuss with your classes and with other people who complete your questionnaire their ratings and opinions. Ask whether they are willing to talk as a group with you about how your teaching might be better and also what they especially like about it. Such a discussion can put comments and recommendations in good perspective and give you a chance to explain why you are teaching what you are teaching and how—both essential to the motivation of most students.

■ In discussion, don't be defensive. If you are, you won't get a useful evaluation. Listen, and listen well. Then, if there's something to explain, explain it and ask for reactions to your explanation.

■ Take the evaluations of your students seriously but not with the reverence that should be reserved for profound truth. You may have good reasons for persisting in methods and with materials that your students do not yet appreciate but that they will come to understand and even respond favorably to. Don't feel obliged to try to follow every suggestion, even though all should be respectfully considered.

■ Every couple of months or so, and especially at midterm and year's end, try to remove yourself from your own teaching and, taking the stance of a tough observer, rate yourself on every item of the questionnaire. After all, you probably know more about your teaching than anyone else.

Another kind of evaluation is one designed to assess a given unit, a short elective course, or even a semester- or year-long course. The form is completed by students. Because they always want to know how the evaluation "came out," it is a good idea, after tabulating their replies, to write out a concise statement of what these contained, what you learned from them, and what changes you expect to make as a result. After reading this to the class for comment, you can share it with a colleague or two or with your supervisor, department head, division head, or principal to get their ideas and perspective on the question and to compare their judgment with yours.

Evaluation for teachers of lower grades can be somewhat simpler in form, especially when pupils are involved. Don't forget that even first and second graders can benefit from a chance to express in writing their opinions about what they are doing in school. A simple checklist is probably better than a form that requires a lot of writing. Basically, what you want to know is: What is good? What isn't so good? How do you feel about what goes on? What should be changed?

Other kinds of evaluation

Because it is probably best for teachers and administrators to devise their own ways and forms for evaluating teacher performance, no detailed samples are given here. Instead, here are a few comments about various kinds of evaluation.

It is important that performance evaluation be done *with* you, the teacher, not *at* you by a form-bearing, capital-E evaluator. Therefore, from the very start, find out what the school's evaluation procedures are and get yourself involved.

One kind of evaluation form asks for a general evaluation of a teacher's work, most suitable to be completed both by the teacher and by the department head or supervisor, the head of the division or the school, or other administrators. Such an evaluation might include questions on a teacher's effectiveness with students, colleagues, and in the life of the school, as well as the teacher's helpfulness and influence in and out of school. This kind of evaluation provides the basis of a review of a teacher's work when teacher and principal, or other supervisor, meet each year to discuss contract and other arrangements, or simply in a scheduled, thorough evaluative conference. If your school uses an evaluation form, get a copy of it early in the year, for you should know by what criteria your work is being evaluated.

A few more suggestions

Before moving on to talk about evaluating your school, I have a few final suggestions to offer on the evaluation of your teaching.

■ Invite a colleague or your principal to visit your class. If your experience is like mine, you have had much less visiting and advice than you would like. Often administrators are embarrassed to pop in on your class for fear of making you nervous. If they know that you welcome their visits, they will find it much easier to come and make comments afterwards. When you invite them, ask them to stay on for a few minutes, if time permits, to discuss what they observed. If they can't, try to find a time later on.

■ Administrators are often so busy with their own tasks that they are likely to say, with the best intentions, "Sure, I'd be glad to visit your class sometime," but just not get around to it. So, in addition to expressing a general desire to be visited, occasionally ask for a visit to a specific class, one you expect to be especially interesting, or one that you are having problems with and need some advice about. Don't worry about exhibiting your weaknesses. The very fact that you ask for a visit and an assessment of the situation is a sign of strength that will be taken as such.

■ If teachers from your school, teachers from other schools, parents, or any other people visit your class, give them a chance to express their views on what they have seen. You can learn a great deal, even from untrained observers, and it helps you to keep in touch.

■ When you are feeling strong, look at your own work—maybe after an especially good or bad class or day—and ask yourself, "What was good? What was bad?" Or, as Abbie Hall says, in Hint 53, "Ask yourself 'Would I like to go to school to such a teacher as I am?'"

■ If you have the courage and the equipment available, have one of your classes videotaped. It can be a real eye-opener to see yourself and your students in action. The less of a big deal it can be, the better.

■ If there is no way to videotape your class, get a tape recorder and let it run the whole time, preferably without telling your students, and then listen carefully to the evidence.

■ Be sure to look at the standardized test results of your class, both as a group and student by student, to see whether by these fallible but not useless measures your students are making progress.

■ Have a suggestion box so that students can tell you what they think when moved to do so. Steel yourself for the usual number of silly, or even mean, comments that may come along with the valuable ones.

■ Take a university or college course or help arrange for an in-service workshop, seminar, or lecture at your school on some basic subject and measure your own work against what you learn. Especially useful are courses in the psychology of learning, teaching methods, tests and measurement, and your own subject field.

■ Arrange for you and a group of colleagues all to read the same book or article and then come together to discuss it. From such activity often comes excellent evaluation of your teaching, a strong stimulus to do better, and yet another occasion for staying in touch.

23.

Testing and Evaluating Your School

We have considered how to get your own teaching evaluated and how to benefit from it. What about an even larger question: How do you evaluate a school and its performance? You may want to do this to help improve it, to decide whether to keep working in it, or, if you are looking for a job, to decide whether to choose a certain school, or school system, to teach in. Accreditation—the long, important exercise that schools, both public and private, go through to improve or be officially recognized—is beyond our scope here. This chapter is simply about your own evaluation of a school, with or independently of your colleagues.

The true measure of a school

The head of a well-known, highly respected school, in speaking to a conference of principals and teachers in whom he found a tendency toward smugness, said, "We don't have good schools, we have good students. Our students are so able and highly motivated that they can hardly help succeeding, no matter what their schools are like. The real measure of the excellence of a school is not how many honors its students win when they graduate, or what highly selective colleges they are accepted by, but rather how effectively the school has helped its students to become more highly motivated, more highly skilled, more competent people than they were, and has increased their ability and determination to become good citizens who use the strengths they have to lead more productive and satisfying lives than they would have done had they not attended the school. *What has the school done to strengthen the students it enrolls?* That is the question."

He went on to point out that many schools that are seldom praised, except in their own communities, are probably doing a far better and more difficult job than highly selective schools or schools in prosperous middle and upper class areas. The true measure should be what the school does rather than the quality of students it selects or has fed to it selectively.

Some schools, inspired by excellent principals and flexible, skilled, committed teachers, are able to take on the least promising students and cause them to learn and develop amazingly well — students from broken or single-parent homes, students whose communities neither honor nor exemplify any kind of scholarship, students whose living conditions make it hard for them to do the sort of reading and writing and thinking and planning that are needed for good schoolwork, students whose parents set few good examples and cannot or do not choose to afford to supply them with the simplest necessities of learning, students who have nothing to look back to with pride and little to look forward to with hope. Schools that work well with students in circumstances like these deserve renown and praise. Until relatively recently, we knew little or nothing about them.

Measuring a school by test results

All too often newspapers and communities evaluate schools simply by the scores their pupils make on standardized tests: tests of the ability to read, write, reckon, and reason — the "basics." People applaud the back to basics, no-frills, workbook and drill curriculums that raise those scores.

Well, it is easy enough to raise test scores, but in a way that does little to improve the real skills of students and does not make them, in any lasting way, better readers, writers, spellers, figurers, or thinkers. The way to do this — and many schools are busy doing it — is to analyze the items on standardized tests and then drill students on these types of item. Teach for the tests and forget the rest; teach how to take tests, and teach it over and over; set up special schools for problem children so that you get only those who want to be there and are ready to cooperate; you are permitted to dismiss anyone who isn't; require students to dress according to a code, always to be respectful; be suspicious of students who ask searching questions; and drill, class, drill! In a school that does these

156

things test scores may go up, in the short run, and the school will be praised, even though students' real knowledge and skills increase only in the narrowest and most fragile sense, and they certainly will not be prepared for college, for any but the most routine work, or for life.

A real-life example of this kind of schooling may be found in the second-grade classroom in which the teacher, firm in her ideas of proper progression in learning arithmetic, asked the class, "All right, children, what numbers between 1 and 10 can be divided by 2?"

Some hands went up, and the teacher called on Jane, who answered, eagerly, "7."

The teacher's face clouded. "Janie," she said scornfully, "how can 7 be divided by 2?"

"That's easy," said Jane. "Seven divided by 2 is 3½."

Wherewith the teacher said, "All right, Jane. If you're going to be smart, you may leave the room."

Does your school encourage thinking? That's a good evaluative question.

Another story takes place in a Sunday school. The preacher was teaching the small children before the main church service. To liven things up, he decided to ask a riddle: "What has a bushy tail, climbs trees, and stores nuts for the winter?"

After a pause, one boy timidly raised his hand. When called upon, he answered, "Well, I know the answer is supposed to be Jesus, but it sure sounds like a squirrel to me."

Does your school encourage that kind of daring realism? Another good evaluative question.

However, I should re-emphasize that schools, in order to avoid wishful thinking and to inform themselves and their communities about how well they are doing, and to help point up academic areas that need work and changes in the curriculum that may be required, should indeed measure the performance of their students by nationally named, widely accepted tests.

Evaluating a school on values

A principal job of schools should be to promote sound values, but students should never be marked or graded on their values, which are their own business. It is desirable, nevertheless, to examine an entire school for values and to make an honest effort to see how well it is promoting them.

The six values named below are ones that are acceptable to almost everyone in a democratic society and that all schools should be encouraged to promote. There is nothing startling about them; in fact, they are so unstartling that we often forget them, but they do provide a good measure for evaluation. Rather than accept these ready-made, ready-stated six, a faculty, or a community, would do well to try to formulate its own statement of values in its own words and then encourage all school people—students, teachers, administrators, and boards of trustees or boards of education—to measure their work against these agreed-upon values.

1. *Information.* Correct information—the facts—is always better than ignorance or rumor. Sound information is necessary for sound thinking and responsible action. People get into trouble not because of what they know but because of what they don't know.

2. *Responsibility.* Being responsible means knowing the consequences of what you do—consequences for yourself and for others, present consequences and future consequences. Irresponsibility is the result of not knowing the consequences or of choosing to act without regard for the consequences of your actions.

3. *Control.* Human beings are powerful creatures. We have the power of thought, of language, of muscle, of sex, of invention. We also exercise the power over things we have discovered or made, like fire, automobiles, and weapons. We should be in control of these powers, not let them control us.

4. *Consideration.* In our thoughts and actions, we should be considerate and caring not only of our own needs, feelings, and welfare but of those of others as well. To be considerate of others, we need to be able to imagine and put ourselves in their shoes that we can better try to learn what they may need and want and take it into account.

5. *Communication.* We need to be able to exchange ideas, information, and feelings with others. Only thus can we understand one another and, in this way, test our own ideas. Communication involves both giving and receiving. The skills of communication should have high priority among those things that are taught in schools.

6. The infinite worth of each person. To feel the worth of others, we need first to feel our own worth. Self-respect is the beginning of respect for others. The opposite of the feeling of self-worth and respecting the worth of others is expressed by a fifteen-year-old boy who dropped out of school and refused to go back. When asked why, he said, "The teacher looked at me as if I was a nothing."

A valuable exercise in evaluating any school is for the faculty, or groups of teachers, to sit down together and look hard at their school – their own work, curricular and extracurricular activities – and to discuss them in the light of the values suggested above. Some questions on their agenda might be these.

Values and Questions for Discussion
[Following the statement of values]

1. Do we understand what these values mean? Do we agree with them? Should some be modified, discarded, or restated? Should some be added? Do any of them involve imposing values on people against their convictions or will?

2. How do our curriculum and activities and methods of teaching strengthen commitment to these values in the lives of our students? Do any aspects of these things weaken that commitment?

3. What part do our counseling and guidance activities play in developing these values?

4. Can we think of specific incidents, events, programs, comments, and remarks that illustrate in a striking manner the good job or the bad job that our school is doing in developing these values?

5. What changes do we need to make in order to promote these values better?

Some additional suggestions

Here are some more suggestions for involving teachers and others in the school as well as outsiders in evaluating the school.

■ The first four chapters talk about order, interest, spirit, and discipline. All of these can be used as criteria to evaluate the work and life of a school. Why not have the faculty, or a group of teachers, read one of these chapters and then discuss it in relation to the school's own realities?

■ Schools tend to evaluate only new programs, courses, or activities, not the old, tried, and perhaps true. At times a school should call up for evaluation the most firmly established aspects of its work and program in the same way that every item is scrutinized in the course of zero-based budgeting—abolish the item, give valid reasons for re-establishing it, and set new limits or goals.

■ Be careful of excessively favorable evaluations of new programs, whose success may spring principally from the creative energy of experiment, not content. As one not entirely cynical critic once said, "All educational experiments are doomed to succeed."

■ Take a major area of the school and have the entire school look at it. The area can be subject or skill (reading, mathematics, foreign language, science, physical education) or a grade or set of grades (grades 4-6, kindergarten and grade 1, the eighth grade, senior year). Such an evaluation can be enlightening both for those who work directly in the activity, who could use an independent, outside look at what they are doing, and for those who know little about the activity and whose teaching may be enriched by what they learn about another aspect of the school.

■ You as a teacher can help initiate the evaluation of your school by making an appointment to talk with the principal or other person in authority about any area that concerns you and you think needs evaluation. Most administrators welcome teachers who bring fundamental questions to them, rather than sudden crises or gripes; they are likely to take up your concern and help work out plans for evaluation. Emphasis should be on what is working well, what needs to be improved, and, specifically, how it can be improved.

■ Take a look at the performance of the head of the school, or the head of your section of the school. If you are an administrator reading this book, you can look at yourself, or even ask a few teachers and other colleagues on the staff to think about your performance and talk it over with you. Here are six criteria for judging the performance of a school head.

Is she skilled in educational leadership and in business management—the basics of budgeting and finding funds? Does she maintain a good balance of time spent in both areas?

Does he know the curriculum of the school and some of the main curricular developments going on in education? Can he, working with others, establish clear academic goals?

Does she move about the school, up and down halls, in and out of classrooms, sufficiently to be in touch with the climate of the school and "what's happening"?

Is he generally supportive of the faculty, and does he pass on both praise and criticism directly to those who need it and make himself available to talk about these things?

Does she make sure that school rules are clear, well known, and fairly administered, without undue emphasis on penalties and punishment?

Does he organize the school in a way that makes teachers free to teach—instruct, discuss, assign, deal with papers—within a sufficiently definite and coordinated curriculum, and without having to spend a high proportion of their time on filling out forms?

■ If you are a teacher thinking about taking a job in another school or another school system, or an expert in an area of subject matter who is thinking about becoming a teacher, how do you evaluate a school to know whether it is the one for you?

Read everything the school or the school system says about itself: philosophy or statement of purpose; school rules; the curriculum; the list of the school's staff; the budget, if published; evaluation forms; salary or benefits system and how it works; and a statement on how the school is governed.

Visit the school for at least one day. Listen, question, and spend time with teachers and students, but don't take up too much of anyone's time. Especially ask teachers whether they like teaching there, students whether they like being pupils there—and why.

Talk with the head or principal of the school to find out how he or she believes the school should be run, is run, and what your contribution to it all might be. Notice what questions are asked of you.

Be sure to visit several classes, especially in your teaching area. If you can do so—and the school may even ask you to—arrange to teach a well-defined lesson to a class similar to classes you may teach if you take a job there.

Go home and ponder all of this for a few days before you make a decision, and visit again if you aren't sure what to decide.

24.

Education for What?

What sorts of people would we like to send forth from our schools? A great and strong variety, of course: people who respect themselves, people who consider others, and people who have their survival skills — reading, writing, reckoning, and reasoning — fully developed. These are the minimum essentials. But I should like to go farther.

We need people who are honest and forthright, sometimes even uncomfortably so. Too many of us tend to be too tactful, too afraid to state our convictions. I don't mean we should encourage brutal forthrightness, for one can tell the truth in a kindly way, and there is even some truth that doesn't need to be spoken at all. But much more often it is better to speak the truth as we see it and to encourage students to do so. We need people who keep trying to communicate, to explain, to say what they think and feel, and to find out what others think and feel.

We need people who will persist in the faith that good will and intelligence, applied by caring, informed people who are moved by their consciences, can improve any situation, whether in a person's life, in a community, or in the world. Schools, properly, work primarily on the brain, but we must remember what anthropologist Loren Eiseley says in *Not Man Apart:* "The need is not really for more brains, the need is now for a gentler, a more tolerant people than those who won for us against the ice, the tiger, and the bear. The hand that hefted the axe, out of the same old blind allegiance to the past, fondles the machine gun just as lovingly. It is a habit man will have to break to survive, but the roots go very deep." We need people who can use their brains—with clarity, gentleness, and tolerance. We need "a different voice."

We need people who take evil, wrongdoing, and injustice personally when these are done to others and who react also when these are done to them. We should train our students to get involved in trying to right injustice, not to pass it by on the other side. We want people who have a chronic social conscience.

We need people who are willing to be unpopular or in the minority, not just for the fun of it, but because what the majority of people are doing so often needs criticism and improvement. But such an attitude should be held without self-righteousness. We need people who will admit that they are wrong.

We need people who, if they have privileges—material, social, mental, physical—feel uncomfortable unless these privileges and powers are harnessed to use for others. A good education is a debt that can be repaid only by the gift of self.

We need people who are not just tolerant of those who are different but who appreciate them, who go out of their way to cross barriers, whether economic, social, religious, racial, or national.

We need people whose loyalty is primarily to the world, not to the nation, for we have reached a point where we must see the welfare of all human beings as inextricably mixed. At the same time, the place we need people to act and work for improvement is where they actually find themselves. It may be interesting to consider what the Chinese, the Russians, the Arabs, the Ugandans, or the Israelis should be doing, but we need people who act primarily as enlightened citizens of their own community, state, and nation. In that sense, we need patriots.

We need people who are religious, not in a sectarian or theological sense, but people who are concerned with the world of the spirit, the world of nonphysical things—love, humor, intellect, sweetness, friendship, loyalty, talk, ideals, and ideas—all things that you can't hold in your hand. *Religio* has to do with binding things together, finding out how they all link together. To develop that sort of religion ought to be the concern of all schools.

We need people who have a sense of unfinishedness. Just as we should know that in any class we do not finish what we begin, so our students should know that their education does not end with school, and we should try to communicate to them a continuing zest for learning and allow them to experience that zest with us. A third grade girl once asked her teacher, "Do I now know half as much as I don't know?" What a wonderful question from the happy state of mind of a third grader, who thought that somehow, someday, she was really going to know everything.

But the truth is that knowledge — all kinds of knowledge, whether factual or spiritual — is like an island in an infinite sea of unknown. The larger the island becomes, the longer is its coastline bordering on the sea of the unknown. The more we know, the more we are in touch with what we don't know. And that is an important attitude for all of us to hold. It can attract us outward and inward, using our powers of heart and mind, to be explorers. May we graduate from our schools joyous, competent explorers!

Index

ability grouping, 79
administration, the, 144-146
"adolescent" thinking, 34
American College Testing Program, 105, 111-112
attention span, 9
authority, establishing and using, 3-4

basics, 27-47
  defined, 28
blaming, 134
books, 88-90
  as teaching devices, 30
  reports on, 89-90

carrels, 84
charts in classroom, 90
cheating, 23-25
  and parents, 24
citizenship, 102
class meetings, 13-15
  and thinking, 13-14
  four-step process, 14-15
class periods, arranging and teaching, 58-62
class size, 77-78
classroom
  routines, 2-3, 58
  special spots and centers in, 83-85
clocks, 59, 100-101
coaching, as type of instruction, 30
College Board tests, 112-113
comments on tests and reports, 126-128
competition, 23

computers, 91
conferences
  individual, 60
  with parents, 133-136
  with students, 19-21, 132-133
contracts with students, 74
correcting and editing papers, 48-51
  shortcuts, 51-53
  system for, 50-51

desks, 85-86
directions, how to give, 39-40
discipline, 41-45
  and freedom, 17
  and punishment, 21-23
  and thinking, 19-20
  defined, 16
  self-discipline, 16-17
discussion, 41-45

encouragement, 49
enthusiasm of teacher, 26
ethics of caring and justice, 35-37
evaluation
  of student performance, 101-136
  of school, 155-161
  of teaching, 149-154
excuses, 20, 21
  and homework, 73

faculty meetings, 144
fairness, 26
  to different types of thinking, 36-37
feelings, acceptance of, 140

fundamentals
  mastery of, 45-47
  steps in mastery, 46-70

Gilligan, Carol, 35-37
grade meetings of parents, 136-137
groups in class, 79-80

head of school, evaluating performance
    of, 160-161
homework, 68-76
honesty, 23, 24
  and teacher's example, 25

independent reading, 90
independent work, 59, 60, 61
instruction, 29-31
  posing questions during, 29-30
  sequence in, 31-34
interest, 8-10, 65
intelligence
  multiple forms of, 105
  tests of (IQ), 105-107

labeling of students, 81
late papers, assignments, 53-54
laughter, 11-12
lecterns, 92
lesson plans, 57-58

marks, 123-129
  and late papers, 53-54
  arguments for, against, 123-124
  on corrected papers, 51
  systems of marking, 126
  when to start, 125-126
master schedule, 97-98
monitoring students, 78-79
moral reasoning, 32-34
motivation, 9-10

order, 1-7
organizing
  groups, 79-80
  materials, 88-96
  people, 77-81
  places, 82-87
  time, 97-100
overhead projectors, 92

parents and homework, 75-76
parent-teacher conferences, 135-136
pass/fail, 123
Piaget, Jean, 31-32
plagiarism, 23-24, 73-74
planning
  a class period, 57-58
  a unit of work, 56
  a year's work, 54-56
pressure, academic, 23
preteaching
  and written work, 51
  and homework, 69-72
privacy of students, 12-13
"problem" students, 108

rank listing, 122
reading, 37-39, 64
relevance, and interest, 10
reports, 130-137
  on younger children, 133-134
  pitfalls to avoid, 131-133
  to students and parents, 130-137
role playing, 141

sarcasm, 12
Scholastic Aptitude Test (SAT), 103,
    111-112
scolding, 12
self-control, 25-26
self-discipline, 16-17
self-respect, 18-19
"sides," choosing, 80
silence, 81
skills, basic, 28
spirit, 11-15
study habits, types of, 65-67
study skills, 62-67
  statement for students about, 63-65

tape recorders, 92
teach-preach-punish syndrome, 13-14
teacher as an example, 25-26
teaching, as distinct from learning, 27
television, 93-95, 141-142
tests and testing, 102-122
  achievement tests, 107
  American College Testing Program (ACT),
    105, 111-112
  and cheating, 24

166

aptitude tests, 105-106
as predictors of success, 103
avoiding bad effects of, 109-110
College Board tests, 112-113
criterion-referenced, 104-105
examinations, 117-119
intelligence tests, 105-107
marking of, 24
multiple-choice, 115-116
norms, 104
objective tests, 103-104
open-book tests, 121
preparing for, 113-114, 118-119
problems of taking, 107-108, 109-110
raw scores, 104
reliable and unreliable tests, 103-104
Scholastic Aptitude Tests (SAT), 103,
111-112
standardized tests, 104, 109-114
teacher-made tests, 115-118
testing terms, 102-104
test results, 120
true-false tests, 116

types of, 104-107
uses of, 102
valid and invalid, 102-103
textbooks, 88-89
time
awareness of, 100-101
free time, 99
how to organize, 97-100
out of school, 98-99
trustees, 146-147
typewriters, 92

values, for a school, 157-159
video equipment, 92
visiting classes, 141-143
visitors, 86-87

worksheets and exercises, 89
workshops, for teachers, 154
writing, benefits of, 48
written work, 48-53
correcting, 48-49
evaluating, 49-50

About the Author

Eric Johnson is a graduate of Germantown Friends School, in Philadelphia, Pennsylvania, and of Harvard College, with an M.A. in teaching from the Harvard Graduate School of Education. He has spent most of his life teaching English, history, and sex education to grades 5-11 in public and independent schools as well as having been head of a junior high school and principal of a K-12 school. He is the author or co-author of thirty-seven books, some of which are *How To Live through Junior High School, Improve Your Own Spelling, Language for Daily Use, Raising Children to Achieve, Love and Sex in Plain Language, The Family Book about Sexuality,* and *How To Live with Parents and Teachers.*